Rousseau in England

Rousseau in England

The Context for Shelley's Critique of the Enlightenment

Edward Duffy

University of California Press
BERKELEY · LOS ANGELES · LONDON

University of California Press
Berkeley and Los Angeles, California

University of California Press, Ltd.
London, England

ISBN 0-520-03695-6

Library of Congress Catalog Card Number 78-57307

for
Felix and Nora Duffy

Contents

Acknowledgments

SEVERAL LIBRARIES have contributed to this study: the New York Public Library, that of the University of California, Santa Barbara, and especially the splendidly open stacks of the Butler Library at Columbia, where for several years I had its abundance of eighteenth- and nineteenth-century periodicals at my fingertips.

A Summer Faculty Fellowship from the Regents of the University of California expedited the work at an important juncture in its metamorphosis from dissertation to book.

The typing of the dissertation was done by Mary Loughran Duffy. In the later stages, I am indebted to the English Department staff at UCSB and especially to Kay Rice and Bill Dell. My warmest thanks, also, to my friend, Barbara Richert.

I owe encouragement, perceptive readings and many detailed suggestions to Howard Schless, Otis Fellows, and Gita May, and to my colleagues, Porter Abbott, Don Pearce, Tom Steiner, and Garrett Stewart. In the struggles of revision, the memory of Karl Kroeber's enthusiasm for the manuscript was an abiding tonic.

The editors at the University of California Press—Udo Strutynski, Alain Henon, and Derek Gallagher—have been both encouraging in spirit and demanding of the letter. I needed both and am grateful.

Although I have tried to record them in my notes, my debts to the community of Shelley scholars and critics are incalculable: without the editorial precision of G. M. Matthews and

Donald Reiman, this book would have been literally impossible, and assistance of a more immediately critical kind came from the writings of Earl Wasserman, R. H. Fogle, and Glenn O'Malley.

Although he does not know it, Peter Gay's massively attended classes at Columbia in the mid-sixties were one of the major impulses toward this book, and although he may not agree with the book's tenor, its indebtedness to those classes is simply too large to be left out. He introduced me to the judgment of Ernst Cassirer and to the excitement of Rousseau.

My largest intellectual debt is also a personal one. Long ago, Carl Woodring suggested the subject of important cultural figures as they are represented in English romantic poetry. Since then, he has impressed upon me (and upon everyone) the political and cultural dimension of romantic poetry. With unfailing patience and support he has read and reread the manuscript of a novice writer who would go his own very slow and tortuous way. The errors and infelicities that remain are, of course, all of my own doing.

Still deeper are the incalculable debts I owe to my wife, Barbara St. John; to my children, Deirdre, Josh, and Ben; and to my parents, to whom I dedicate this book.

Introduction

THE MANY poems of the English romantics that organize themselves around a Greek myth, nonetheless, stay very close to
home. In the respectful but transforming hands of these romantic Hellenists, ancient forms and stories usually become
types relevant to their own immediate situation and pliable to
their own aesthetic and mimetic purposes: the Jupiter of *Prometheus Unbound*, for example, is less the Roman alias of the
supreme Olympian than Milton's divine autocrat and less this
than he is Shelley's embodiment of nineteenth-century
tyranny. Such making free with the gods of Hellas, however, is
not an indulgence peculiar to either romantic or radical. A
general practice in eighteenth- and early nineteenth-century
England, it is, in addition, only half of the poetic license English wordmen claimed for themselves. Complementing the
poet's insinuation of historical referent into ancient fable is the
journalist's trick of heightening historical fact into mythology—
turning Edmund Burke into Demosthenes or Napoleon into
Satan. On October 10, 1794, when the rulers of revolutionary
France translated the remains of Voltaire and Rousseau to the
newly constructed Pantheon, they dramatized a kind of imaginative translation that both specific English poets and general
English opinion would subsequently perform on Napoleon and
the upheavals he incarnated. The English did not deify Napoleon—quite the contrary—but they did repeatedly present him
as the symbolic form in which the age had most clearly expressed itself. In short, they mythologized him, elevated him

1

not to a pantheon of value but to an ecumenical pantheon of significance, harboring both Milton's Satan and Milton himself, both Olympian and Titan.

This book is the history of how another such legend took his place (or places) in English mythology. It seeks to define and trace the expressive forms into which the English cast the figure of Jean-Jacques Rousseau, and it takes as the climactic text in this progression Shelley's "The Triumph of Life," a poem in which the complexly presented figure of Rousseau becomes Shelley's type for where, in 1822, the European community was, whence it came, and whither it was rushing.

To most Europeans of the second and third decades of the nineteenth century the myth for their time was Napoleon. For Shelley it became Rousseau. What allowed Shelley to redefine his era depended on two assumptions that were the common property of him and his compatriots: that the notorious Rousseau was an all too typical man of the Enlightenment and that the Napoleonic disasters were the inevitable consequence of an Enlightenment ideology wrong headed from the start and most notoriously wrong headed in Jean-Jacques Rousseau. How and why these assumptions became so dominant in England is the subject of my first two chapters. They constitute a biography not of Rousseau as he might have been in himself but as the English forged him into a cultural symbol—the polemical fabrication that the propaganda of Edmund Burke cast into an all but uncrackable mold.

Burke's word on Rousseau has not been the last, however. As dictatorial and rigid as it was, it eventually dissolved into that babel of interpretations a historical perspective shows whirling about Rousseau. For the legions who have written of Rousseau often register less the forces and contours of their subject than the distortions of their own place and time. They translate this putatively influential man into their own terms, and Rousseau the writer often becomes less text than pretext— an unstable compound made to become what alchemicist commentators would have it become. Rousseau has been an especially volatile compound. Driven by prejudice, critical mode, or political allegiance, critics have edited, confused, and distorted bits and pieces of Rousseau, producing a multitude of often contradictory characters: the revolutionary, the collectivist, the individualist, the totalitarian, the sentimentalist, the infidel, the primitivist, the evolutionist, the libertine, the moralist, the rationalist, the romantic, the existentialist, the structuralist. So much obscured by interested criticism, the citizen of Geneva has been further complicated by the intricate interweavings of his life and thought. Polemicists seldom neglect any effective means available to them, and when Rousseau not only lived an eccentric life but voluminously reported it, he gave them a powerful weapon. Hostile critics like Burke have constantly used this Rousseau, naked and without ornament, to discredit anything that could flow from such a polluted source. The faith of the Savoyard priest, the concept of popular sovereignty, the sentiment of *La Nouvelle Héloïse* have all been pronounced as contemptible as the most scabrous episode of the *Confessions*.

With a critical tradition so varied that much of it would have to be misrepresentation, it is essential to ascertain just what notion of Rousseau prevailed in England in the eighteenth and early nineteenth centuries. For that representation is the cultural language within which any utterance of the time must have taken shape, and without a knowledge of the grammar and syntax of that language we cannot even begin to assess what significance specific English writers may have sought to make out of the now symbolic phenomenon called Jean-Jacques Rousseau.

(I am borrowing my metaphor from Ferdinand de Saussure's important distinction: *langue* is "that aspect of language which is social and apart from the individual, *the latter being unable either to create or to modify it*. It exists only by virtue of what one might term the contract established among the members of a community"; *parole* is "by contrast, the deliberate and intelligent act of an individual, an act essential to which are the operations which a given speaker performs on the language code in order that he may use it to express his own individual thoughts."[1] A cultural *langue* and *parole*, however, differ, from their literal counterparts in that [contrary to the italicized phrase] an individual agent like Edmund Burke can and does transform the larger body of conventional significance: George Bernard Shaw could not change English spelling; he could change our notion of Joan of Arc.)

To understand the significance of, for example, Coleridge on Rousseau, it is not enough to read Coleridge's words in a vacuum. One must sense the cultural givens assumed by these words. Only then can one know whether a particular utterance is a restatement of the conventional wisdom or a transforming act of individual intelligence, its significance inhering in the why and how of its deflections from shared cultural myth. Coleridge spoke very authoritatively on Rousseau, but to assess the nature and value of the goods delivered, one has to know whom Coleridge was addressing. One has to know the marketplace of idea and symbol in which he was hawking his wares, the arena in which he was performing. My three final chapters are a review of such performances; the artists are the major figures of English romanticism as they worked either within or upon the givens of the Rousseau myth in England. The chapters progress from the English romantics in general to Shelley in particular, and finally to Shelley's last major poem. I conclude so lengthily on "The Triumph of Life" not only because it was the most concrete and complex instance of Rousseau translated into quasi-mythical significance but also because, given what the history of Rousseau's English reputation reveals, such a detailed act of interpretation seems necessary.[2] The poem's recasting of the conventional Rousseau myth is not unlike what Shelley did to Aeschylus' Prometheus, but the how and why of this recasting (and indeed its very existence) have been neglected by a historical and mythical naiveté sufficiently alive to the Aeschylean presence in *Prometheus Unbound* but not so alert to Shelley's starting point in "The Triumph of Life"—that is, the Rousseau of his time and place, "Rousseau" as inflected by a British accent, circa 1822.

In my effort to reconstruct the English reputation of Rousseau, I have been greatly helped by the work of two French scholars: Jacques Voisine, *J.-J. Rousseau en Angleterre à l'époque romantique* (1956), and Henri Roddier, *J.-J. Rousseau en Angleterre au XVIIIᵉ siècle* (1950). The book that follows does not, however, duplicate their considerable efforts. Roddier's book is a study of the influence of Rousseau the thinker on various English writers—usually minor and often quite specialized. By contrast, I direct my attention to the general and usually unexamined assumptions about Rousseau—the kind of cultural data contained not so much in an English pedagogue's innovative use of Rousseau as in the evolving pattern of emphases to be found in the English reviews of *Émile* and *La Nouvelle Héloïse*. Voisine's study, which covers the same chronological ground as all but my first chapter, is indeed a survey of major English writers and what they wrote about Rousseau. But, that I choose Shelley as my major figure and Voisine chooses Hazlitt results from our different angles of approach to the subject. I do not wish to repeat Voisine's work, that is, give an encyclopedic account of English allusion to Rousseau. What, by contrast, I have tried to render more visible are the lines of cultural force behind the many ways the English had of using "Rousseau" toward their own homemade purposes.

Insensitivity to the world from which an English artist projects himself onto Rousseau may cause one to see an incomplete picture of the Rousseau fashioned by that artist. The politicalized English image of Rousseau being what it was, it is manifestly implausible that someone as political as Shelley would interest himself only in (as Voisine contends) "une partie restreinte de l'oeuvre de Rousseau—essentiellement la *Nouvelle Héloïse*, et, à un moindre degré, les *Rêveries*."[3] But if a focus so narrowly "literary" misses much of Shelley, it does indeed very nicely accord not only with certain preconceptions about the subjectivity of romanticism but also with the explicitly announced limits of Voisine's "sujet qui nous était pratiquement imposé par le choix de la période étudiée: l'action exercée par la personnalité de Rousseau sur la littérature poétique qui naît en Angleterre au lendemain de sa mort."[4] In relation to the "Triumph," the assertion that Shelley cared only about *Julie* and the *Rêveries* may remain plausible only because Voisine is not sufficiently alert to the poem's nature as an epitomized history of European demoralization as seen from post-Napoleonic England. Voisine knows that Rousseau was both political figure and prose poet, but not appreciating the political referent of the poem into which Shelley has inserted Rousseau, he misreads the nature and function of the Rousseau to be found there. He sees Shelley's condensed life of Rousseau only as a "message platonicien," the "symbole d'une quête de l'idée de la beauté."[5] What he does not see is that the "Rousseau" in Shelley's poem is unintelligible if divorced from his implication in the blood, mire, and controversy of recent European experience. In short, this poem literally crammed with history Voisine sees not as a critique of the civilization for which Rousseau is an ambivalent spokesman but rather as a rarefied species of romantic vision. Blind to the large but pointed political import of the "Triumph," he eviscerates Shelley's Rousseau of precisely that historical embodiment by which the romantic poet would make Jean-Jacques the epitome of his age.

That the English wrote extensively about Rousseau—Hazlitt more than most—is what Voisine has conclusively shown. That they used him to their own purposes is my premise, a premise that has as its consequence the close examination of the why and how of Shelley's mythopoeic imagination as applied to Rousseau. Thus the extent and nature of my concluding emphasis not on the confessional memoirs of Hazlitt, Voisine's "nouveau Jean-Jacques," but on the "Triumph of Life," a longer poem that appropriates those tight structures of metaphor and language usually found only in the sonnet, ode, or lyric. Strainingly compact as it may be, the style of Shelley's last poem is the necessary sinew and muscle for the herculean labor of historical revision which he set himself, but such poetic muscularities will seem necessary to Shelley's task—and their anatomy incumbent on the critic—only if one appreciates that Shelley is addressing himself to a veritable Augean stable of false consciousness—a dominant image of Rousseau decades thick at the time, and still being spread around by both the knowing and the unknowing engines of political power in England.

In "The Triumph of Life," Shelley has constructed a poem whose final gesture may be toward "the loftiest star of unascended heaven / Pinnacled dim in the intense inane," but the audience of that poem (the inhabitants of Europe in 1822) cannot help but be the only possible sharers and beneficiaries of his vision. The "Triumph" is a poem public in kind and clarifying in intent. It seeks to describe the origins and future of a community, and it contrives its prophetic sweep on the energy of pointed historical analysis. Its vision does not hover in a private space above reality. Rather it "projects from incision," the incisiveness of an imagination both historical and visionary.[6]

The actuality Shelley was constantly attempting to clarify was the French Revolution, its causes and consequences.[7] He needed to be incisive about it because he was honest enough to acknowledge that twenty-six years after its outbreak, Europe found itself bound into a system of despotism seemingly more alert and effective than the ancien régime. He was acutely aware that the public events that formed the background to his life were constantly being taken as yet another emblem for would-be betterers of the human condition, "[heaping] thousandfold torment on themselves," and there was no lack of analysts to proclaim that such pragmatic failures were but the inevitable consequence of the putative cause of the aborted new order—that is, the ideology of the Enlightenment. Sharing this conventional etiology of the revolution and becoming increasingly estranged from the Enlightenment ethos, Shelley nonetheless did not wish to concede that the impulse of the revolution had been wrong from its inception. He needed to articulate a new basis for the revolution, one which would preserve its essential rightness and account for its acknowledged shortfall; and it was to such uses, inextricably both intimate and public, that he put the Rousseau of his last poem. For, while the Rousseau of the "Triumph" was the stock figure almost universally placed at the source of the revolution, he was also that figure whom a surprised Shelley had come to recognize as something more than a *philosophe*. From that surprise there grew in Shelley's mind the possibility of a different etiology for the revolution, one that would be conventional in that it placed Rousseau at its origin, individual in that it defined Rousseau as strikingly different from the notion of him canonized by general English opinion.

Shelley's surprise at the Rousseau whom he eventually discovered depended on a complex of assumptions which was the common cultural property of his English contemporaries. His surprise would not have been a surprise had it not gone counter to these general assumptions and had he not shared them. These assumptions make up the hitherto uncharted cultural context of the "Triumph," and it is their retrieval that necessitates the apparently fractured structure of this book—its first four chapters of historical reconstruction and its final chapter of literary analysis. I would ask my reader, however, to conceive the book as a series of narrowing concentric circles, a progress inward from the general and the assumed to the specific and the attentive, an effort to define the conventional Rousseau with which Shelley's poem began but against the resistance of which it sought to educe a quite different figure—the "poet" whom Shelley pronounced "the greatest man since Milton."[8]

1

Rousseau's English Reputation, 1751–1778

Rousseau's first English appearance was a translation of the *Discours sur les sciences et les arts*, published by William Bowyer in June of 1751—just six months after the French edition.[1] In a brief preface Bowyer dismisses the ideas of Rousseau and insists that he offers them only because of their great "singularity."[2] The Academy of Dijon, he assures us, awarded Rousseau first prize not for the sentiments expressed but for the eloquence of expression. The *Monthly Review* had similar praise for this "complete master of the declamatory art" and similar contempt for his sophistical opinions.[3]

While the *Discours sur les sciences et les arts* appeared almost immediately in two different English translations,[4] the comparably eloquent and much more important *Discours sur l'origine de l'inégalité parmi les hommes* had to wait seven years for an English version.[5] Prior to 1762, of course, the second discourse in the original French was not unknown. French books found their way across the Channel quickly and easily: Rousseau's *Oeuvres diverses*,[6] in which the discourse was included, had been formally imported by the bookseller, Nourse, in January of 1758,[7] and even before that, the young Adam Smith, in the short-lived *Edinburgh Review*, had devoted five pages to it in a review of continental literature.[8] It was not, however, until

1763, that (as James Boswell relates) the second discourse became a fashionable topic in London.[9] When, four years before, the *London Chronicle* had presented excerpts of the English translation of Rousseau's *Lettre à d'Alembert sur les spectacles*, it had indeed introduced the author as someone already well known, but only for his first discourse, his *Dissertation sur la musique moderne*, and his music articles in the *Encyclopédie*. The newspaper did not see fit to make any mention of the second discourse.[10]

The place of the *Lettre à d'Alembert sur les spectacles* in the formation of Rousseau's English reputation has not been sufficiently appreciated. Roddier gives the letter only three pages and concludes that it "sera de beaucoup le moins cité parmi ses livres les plus connus."[11] That the *Lettre sur les spectacles* would be infrequently cited is true, but the contrary is true for its first English appearance in 1759 when it was reviewed at length by the *London Chronicle*, the *Monthly Review*, the *Critical Review*, the *London Magazine*, and Burke's *Annual Register*.[12] During 1759, the *Annual Register* reviewed only six books. One of them was the *Lettre sur les spectacles*.

In d'Alembert's argument for a theater in the city of Calvin, Rousseau sensed a threat to Genevan virtue. Springing to the defense of his community, the citizen responded with passionate descriptions of an idealized Geneva, animated by virtue and denying pleasures for a duty it had come to love. In Rousseau's hands the French theatre and its proposed introduction into Geneva served as a focus for the confrontation of what he took to be two opposed sets of social values—the one corrupt, effeminate, and enslaved; the other simple, manly, and free.

English commentators recognized the author of the *Lettre* for what indeed he was: the advocate of a strenuous public and private morality, the champion of simple manners, and the inheritor of an ancient republican tradition cherished as the nurse of virtue. But, while appreciative of Rousseau's good intentions and even awestruck by his eloquence, Englishmen were not to be stampeded into assent. Eloquently sublime Rousseau may have been; reasonably practical he most certainly was not. To the *Monthly Review*, Rousseau was "too implicit an admirer of antique simplicity to adapt his scheme to the age in which he lives." To others his morality was "too rigid," his virtue of an austerity "pushed to an unsociable fierceness." The English possessed very little solid information on Rousseau, but to such a person as they conceived him to be—a virtuous recluse pursuing a simple life far away from the corruptions of polite society—they were favorably disposed. The preface to a translation of the first discourse admiringly relates a story illustrative of the citizen's sincerity. The Duc d'Orleans, a would-be patron, had paid Rousseau 2,000 *livres* for some music-copying work, but Rousseau, "adhering strictly to his favorite Maxim that what a Man enjoys more than is necessary for the Support of Life is Luxury, consequently culpable," promptly returned all of the money save the sum due and owing of six shillings.[13]

The *Lettre sur les spectacles* was immediately popular, and it was only the brilliant success of *La Nouvelle Héloïse* which eclipsed it. Total eclipse, however, is a far too simplistic statement of the case. If it is true that the novel replaced the tract, it is an equal and complementary truth that the tract prepared the way for the novel. For it is this sternly moral work, written by *un citoyen de Genève* in defense of his homeland's Roman virtues and against French corruption, which influenced decisively the way in which the British public received and understood *La Nouvelle Héloïse*.

Somewhat beclouding Rousseau's good image were the charges that he really did have an absurd preference for the savage state of nature, and that he was a recluse of the gloomy, misanthropic type, a modern Diogenes.[14] While material for these charges could be found in the first discourse's critique of civilized refinement, they were more likely to derive from a reading of the second discourse. Although the latter was not widely known, it was not totally unavailable, and it is reasonable to suppose that a literate Englishman at least knew of its existence. Even with the text in front of us, caricature has often obscured our understanding of this work; on such slight acquaintance as the English possessed before 1762, caricature could very easily have preempted accurate knowledge. And there was no lack of caricature. The English public was probably vaguely and derivatively aware of Voltaire's remark that reading this "new libel on the human race" made him want to crawl about on all fours.[15] They were certainly and immediately cognizant of Palissot's similar characterization of a savage and misanthropic Rousseau in *Les Philosophes*:[16] the celebrated scene where Crispin-Rousseau appears on all fours, munching a head of lettuce, was reproduced in its entirety in the *Monthly Review*.[17]

It would appear, then, that there did exist in English consciousness some faint apprehension of Rousseau as savage and Rousseau as Diogenes. But these apprehensions were all the more obscure because they could be so easily incorporated into the master image of Rousseau as a latter-day Cato, an austere critic of the luxury and refinement of his age. And so from the voluminous pages of *La Nouvelle Héloïse* the Englishmen of 1761 extracted a moralist: Rousseau leading the assault against luxury into its very citadel, Rousseau imagining a rural community that was the moral antithesis of Parisian sophistication.

II

La Nouvelle Héloïse was first published in Amsterdam, November 1760—only a month before the *Monthly Review* announced the novel's English importation by the firm of Becket and de Hondt.[18] The *Monthly's* notice also included the announcement of a forthcoming translation. The periodical knew whereof it spoke, for the first half of the novel was quickly translated and on the booksellers' shelves by April. The notice of publication in the *London Chronicle* lists Ralph Griffiths as the bookseller, in addition to Becket and de Hondt.[19] Griffiths was the publisher of the *Monthly Review*, and William Kenrick, the translator of *La Nouvelle Héloïse*, was one of his regular writers, working for the *Monthly* from February 1758, to December 1765.[20] It seems likely that Griffiths was the prime mover in what was essentially a business venture—the speedy translation of what was likely to be a best-seller—a novel of broad, popular appeal from the pen of a not unknown French writer. Judging from the volume of prepublication notices and samples, one cannot help but suspect that there was someone aggressively publicizing the new translation. The *London Chronicle* alone contained nineteen selections within eight months, many of them two entire folio pages in the eight-page triweekly. In all, I count thirty-three accounts of *La Nouvelle Héloïse*—most of them long excerpts in the *London Chronicle*, the *Monthly*, the *Critical*, the *Gentleman's Magazine*, and the *London Magazine*.

Introducing the French novel, both the *Monthly* and the *Critical*[21] made explicit reference to Richardson, whose novels had demonstrated that a literate and expanding middle class desired and would support a literature that mirrored the life it led and inculcated the moral values it honored. Rousseau, the reviewers asserted, would be found appealing, because, like Richardson, he had accomplished the affecting narration of ordinary events conceivable as the actions of ordinary people. The *Gentleman's Magazine* saw *La Nouvelle Héloïse* as a book "in which the various subjects that are most interesting in private life are treated in a masterly manner."[22] The *Critical Review* wrote that in this new work Rousseau "lays the philosopher aside, and mixes in the cheerful ways of men, paints with the most luxuriant imagination, and interests every passion with the most bewitching art."[23]

But if it is true that the genre of *La Nouvelle Héloïse* is middle-class idyll, one should not ignore what was equally evident to Rousseau's contemporaries: the aggressively political tone with which he chose to depict the pleasures of the common life. For, in an expansion of the antithesis of the *Lettre sur les spectacles*, *La Nouvelle Héloïse* juxtaposes the ideal happiness of Clarens with the "great world" of Paris. Although St. Preux's Parisian exile occurs only as an interlude in the main story and although it comprises only seven letters, all seven of these digressions found their way into the English press, one appearing no less than four times.[24] These English excerpts of *Eloisa* set up a pattern of confronting social ideals even starker than what might be discerned from the novel itself. Aside from St. Preux's dispatches from Paris, the English press printed only five other letters from the first half of the novel. One of these is an obvious foil to the corruptions of Paris, and just as obviously is it a celebration done in the manner of the *Lettre sur les spectacles*. Its locus is the Swiss region of le Valais—an idyllic scene of natural happiness and freedom where even the air is purer. All the other four excerpted pieces are in a similarly didactic vein, two of them being trenchant criticisms of aristocratic mores.

Rousseau's second and belated preface to *La Nouvelle Héloïse* (a great part of which was reproduced in the *London Chronicle*) makes explicit the novel's social ideal. Deploring most "romances" as fraudulent ads for the great world of Paris, it offers *La Nouvelle Héloïse* as a persuasion toward precisely the opposite social effect:

> to convince mankind that in rural life there are many pleasures which they know not how to enjoy; that these pleasures are neither so insipid nor so gross as they imagine; that a sensible man, who should retire with his family into the country, and become his own farmer, might enjoy more rational felicity, than in the midst of the amusements of a great city.[25]

Of the ten excerpts the *London Chronicle* printed from the second half of the novel, fully eight of them described what the newspaper entitled the "domestic economy" of Clarens, an economy the reiterated simplicities of which were, point for point, foiled by the sophistications of the dominant French culture.[26]

Only one voice was raised in dissent against the general Rousseaumania. In September and October of 1761, three of England's most popular monthlies printed a prickly little satire supposedly from the pen of Voltaire.[27] Actually the real author of the *Prédiction tirée d'un vieux monument* was Charles Bordes, a *philosophe* and friend of Voltaire, who had previously disputed the thesis of Rousseau's first discourse. The satire's universal attribution to Voltaire made it more popular than it might have been otherwise, and Edmund Burke included it in the *Annual Register* for 1761. Far from being ecstatic over *la vie champêtre*, Bordes ridiculed the novel's rural simplicities as fussy dottering over pointless trivialities like the layout of a provincial garden or the cutting of hemp. The *Prophecy* caused only a slight eddy in the great current of English admiration for *La Nouvelle Héloïse*, but it is interesting for the truly prophetic character of its attitude toward Rousseau. Its burlesque presentation of Jean-Jacques as a wild prophet come from the shores of Lake Geneva to bring the French to judgment, while it maliciously confirms the extraordinary eloquence of Rousseau's anti-Parisian pen, hints at the less-than-generous estimate of his mental competence which later events were to establish as dogma in England.

Bordes's most telling charge against Rousseau was the one most opposite to his reputation as a sublime moralist, and it did not go totally unrecognized by the English public. It is difficult to believe that Bordes should call what might aptly be described as a whole duty of middle-class man "a book which inspires vice." But such is the fact, and one should not forget that *Pamela* was the object of similar insinuations and from no less perceptive a reader of novels than Henry Fielding. What *Pamela* and *La Nouvelle Héloïse* had in common was that they were both novels of sentiment, and "sentiment" in the eighteenth-century lexicon was a word extraordinary in the ambiguity of its usage. To some, affectivity was the instrumentality for the most orthodox percepts, while to others it was a feeble pliancy unable to sustain any kind of moral purposiveness. We are indebted to Ernst Cassirer for his demonstration that Rousseau's most important and most consistent understanding of sentiment was as an immediate intuition of moral fitnesses, felt rather than excogitated.[28] Rousseau himself wrote that one should not "[confondre] les penchans secrets de notre coeur qui nous égarent, avec ce dictamen plus secret, plus interne encore, qui réclame et murmure contre ces décisions intéressées, et nous ramène en depit de nous sur la route de la vérité. Ce sentiment intérieur est celui de la nature elle-même.[29] But this is a fine distinction, as difficult in theory as in practice. The heat of Rousseau's passion for the morally beautiful, and especially his incarnation of it in a physical beauty—one who had not stinted at *les dernières faveurs*—inevitably suggested, even to the favorably disposed, that there was a great deal of sensuality lurking behind so much fine sentiment. But to the mass of Rousseau's enchanted admirers, such a criticism seemed no more than a petty cavil. It would become dominant only when personal antagonism toward the author of *La Nouvelle Héloïse* made it seem incredible that such a man could be stirred by anything more exalted than sensual passion. For the moment at least, the Rousseau given most play in England was the trenchant moralist who, having written the *Lettre sur les spectacles*, bettered that performance in *La Nouvelle Héloïse*. He was the incorruptible who had written to and against d'Alembert, to and against the *Encyclopédie*, to and against Paris, to and against all of what Voltaire had celebrated as *le mondain*.

III

As the 1760s began, "ingenious" was the established and almost obligatory epithet for Rousseau. He was a man "peculiar and original in everything."[30] The typical English response to him was a complexity that refrained from bothering itself into a perplexity—a comfortable simultaneity of disregard for Rousseau's judgements and admiration for his writings. As the *Critical Review* would say of *Émile*:

> Mr. Rousseau can handle the most beaten topic with novelty, and throw new light on subjects which have been thought exhausted. As if he enjoyed a peculiar sensation, every object strikes his mind in a very uncommon manner, and hence it is possible that his writings will be admired as the effusions of genius, while his precepts will be neglected as the effects of caprice and affectation.[31]

Surrendering themselves to the beauties of *La Nouvelle Héloïse*, the English had scarcely seen the novel as anything other than an unqualified and very moral "effusion of genius." Approaching *Émile* with similar expectations, they at first saw only what they very eagerly wanted to see—*Émile* as a variation on the theme of middle-class idyll. The *London Chronicle* printed excerpts urging mothers to nurse their own children because (as Rousseau said) "the charms of domestic life [were] undoubtedly the most powerful antidote against corruption of manners."[32]

From the fifth book, the *London Magazine* excerpted a passage on the different kinds of compatibility necessary for a successful marriage.[33] This, the final book of *Émile*, is now generally regarded as a reactionary and antifeminist fantasy that is anything but essential to the program for mankind outlined by *Émile*. The eighteenth-century English, however, thought so highly of the fifth book that they gave its heroine a place in the title of the English translation. To the English reading public, Rousseau's new book was not *Émile* but *Emilius and Sophia*.[34] Glowing in its praise of almost the entire work, the *Critical Review* waxed incandescent at the sentimental novella of Sophia's union with Émile:

He expresses every wish and fear of the amiable pair with the most glowing pencil and voluptuous coloring of ardent passion and immaculate innocence. All the feelings of exquisite sensibility are freely painted, without a single touch that provokes impurity or alarms delicacy. Nature is copied with such heat of enthusiasm, as declares our author's heart susceptible of the soft passion, and intimates that he has sacrificed both to the Loves and Graces. His own passions and his readers [*sic*] are equally at his command; in the midst of a dry didactic discourse, he twitches the heart and bedews the face with sympathetic tears.[35]

As is indicated by the conjecture made here about Rousseau's personal sensibility, Jean-Jacques was imagined mainly as he had revealed himself in his writings. Little notice had as yet been taken either of the eccentric man behind the writings or of that dangerous heretic whose works the Parlement of Paris had already condemned "to be burnt by the common hangman."[36]

But with Rousseau fleeing from one European proscription to another, newspapers would soon carry more accounts of his misfortunes than literary reviews would of his books, and in the formation of his reputation personal fate would soon begin to compete with literary production. The *Monthly Review* offered *Émile* as interesting not only for the fame of its author and the importance of its subject, but also for its "extraordinary notice" and "severe treatment" abroad.[37] With such notoriety as was the immediate fate of *Émile*, there began not only the

shift from Rousseau in his books to Rousseau in the newspapers but also the first movement toward what would eventually become a decisive retreat away from delectation over
Rousseau's prose and into pointed questions about both his
personal and ideological soundness, questions the goad to
which was not so much the detached perusal of Rousseau's
works as the almost weekly bulletins about the fugitive's misadventures—the indictments drawn up against him, his renunciation of Genevan citizenship, and his banishment from one
community after another.[38]

On the continent the original charge against *Émile* had been
religious in nature, the major piece of evidence being the *Profession de foi d'un vicaire savoyard*, an eighteenth-century credo
inserted into *Émile* and composed of one part fervent personal
piety and one part cool scepticism toward the claims of institutional religion. For his panegyrics on Christ as moral teacher
and exemplar, few churchmen were ready to embrace Rousseau as a lost sheep returned from the wolf of the Enlightenment. They chose instead to bear down heavily on the negative
preliminaries of the vicar. Ostensibly religious, the sins of
Rousseau were, in fact, political. Analyzing revelation as nothing more than a fiction useful toward the establishment of
authority, Rousseau demoted sacred dogma into a (now trans-
parent) technique for profane governance. Subsequently, when
Rousseau became both major issue and fiery polemicist in the
factional strife of Geneva, the attendant disorder was seen as
the handiwork of a Rousseau whose published speculations
were as officially heterodox as his personal vagaries were notoriously bizarre.

By 1776, when Rousseau was forced to flee to England, he
had become persona non grata in almost every European capital, and even in constitutional England, some few voices were
beginning to be raised echoing the sentiments and fears of continental authority. A preview of this kind of critical and personal severity may be seen in the reception given the second
discourse, finally translated in 1762. When the *Critical Review*
recommended that the discourse be read "rather as a specimen

of talents than a lesson in philosophy,"[39] the reviewer seemed decidedly more annoyed with absurdities than enchanted with beauties:

In a word, we see a performance, every paragraph of which contradicts the plainest maxims of common sense, . . . and we conclude with regarding the author as a prodigy of genius, misled and infatuated by caprice and the affectation of peculiarity.[40]

Echoing these sentiments, the *London Chronicle* assigned Rousseau to "romances" not in enthusiastic praise but as the limit of his rather frivolous talents:

This writer never did, and never will succeed in any undertaking which requires sound judgment and an accurate spirit of investigation. A man who is carried away by an irregular fancy and a proud spirit of misanthropy, is only fit for writing Romances and Rousseau was never designed by nature for performances of a higher class.[41]

Even the vigor of his prose was soon being held against Rousseau. One still spoke of the "enchantment of words,"[42] but the magic now seemed less celestial than infernal, his verbal facility the only kind of cosmetic that could have forestalled a totally merited contempt for both his character and his opinions.

Since Rousseau's ideas were patently absurd, one sought to explain him not by weighing his reasons but by unearthing their origin in a radical defect of character. By some, Rousseau was conceived to be essentially a child, captivated by the bright lights of his own rhetoric and mistaking for the truth anything that was capable of forceful and original expression. To the less indulgent, his bizarre ideas seemed calculated efforts to distinguish himself by a display of literary and sophistical talent. In July of 1763, before antagonism toward Rousseau had become anything like a dominant attitude, Samuel Johnson gave voice to both variants of such invidious personal analysis. First in a not too irascible mood:

Rousseau, and all those who deal in paradoxes, are led away by a childish desire of novelty. When I was a boy, I used always to choose the wrong side of a debate, because most ingenious things, that is to say, most new things, could be said upon it.[43]

The following morning, Johnson was more severe:

Hume, and other sceptical innovators [the context makes it plain that Rousseau is among them] are vain men, and will gratify themselves at any expence. Truth will not afford sufficient food to their vanity; so they have betaken themselves to errour. Truth, Sir, is a cow which will yield such people no more milk, and so they are gone to milk the Bull.[44]

But as a judge of Rousseau, the often irascible Dr. Johnson was somewhat ahead of his time. The Tory *Critical Review* might brand the author of the *Profession de foi* an ''enemy to society.''[45] Edmund Burke might describe *Émile* as ''impracticable and chimerical'' and positively ''dangerous.''[46] But to most of the insular beneficiaries of the Glorious Revolution, it was only too easy to cast Rousseu as a persecuted Socrates, Europe as an inquisitorial Athens. In the preface to his translation of *Émile* (1762), William Kenrick replied to those who thought Rousseau to possess ''too little respect for received opinions'':

it is the interest, as it should be the pride of a free people to give him a candid hearing . . . it is to be hoped, that England will be the last country in the world wherein the friends of truth or liberty will be restrained from thus exercizing their talents for the service and improvement of mankind.[47]

The idealization of Rousseau as martyred witness to truth and liberty is nowhere more apparent than in the excited state of mind and soul of James Boswell as in December 1764 he makes a pilgrimage to Rousseau's refuge at Motiers. Extreme in his invocation to ''eloquent and amiable Rousseau,'' Boswell nonetheless typifies the pleasant moral fantasies the British were apt to spin around a writer who, personally unknown to them, could yet be regarded as the noble victim of a tyrannical and bigoted continent. Boswell is important because his is probably the last fully articulated response to Rousseau that remains uncomplicated by the unattractive facts and would-be facts of Rousseau's personal history. The hyperbolic strokes of Boswell's portraiture vividly reveal the kind of veneration accorded Rousseau before his battering by controversy.

To the master of sentiment, living a simple, retired life in the hills of Neuchâtel, Boswell was careful to introduce himself "as a man with a feeling heart." Even more significant was the kind of moral results that Boswell expected from Rousseau's sentimental energies. He hoped to take leave of Rousseau with a firm hold on "two or three simple and noble principles": "O charitable philosopher! I beseech you to help me. My mind is weak but my soul is strong. Kindle that soul, and the sacred fire shall never be extinguished."[48] In the eyes of authority, Rousseau had committed sacrilege; but to Boswell the Genevan's teaching was religious in nature. Indeed, Boswell singled out for piety that very profession of faith which so many spokesmen for the Church had condemned. Agonizing with guilt before a Calvinist God, Boswell represents a significant European group, the members of which had anticipated the vicar's corrosive analysis of revelation but not his apparent ability still to lay claim to the title of Christian. Boswell expressed the gratitude of an entire generation when he said, "I would never have had the agreeable ideas I possess of the Christian religion, had I not read 'The Savoyard's Creed'."[49]

But, as we have seen, neither Rousseau's consolation for those tottering in their faith nor his eloquent praise of the Gospels forestalled an ecclesiastical onslaught. With attention drawn almost exclusively to the negations of Rousseau's creed, the authorities' claim that he meant to destroy Christendom began to appear ever more plausible, and Rousseau's explicit replies to such as the Archbishop of Paris further fixed the public eye on a heterodoxy that was beginning to scandalize even the liberal *Monthly*. Reviewing the *Lettres de la montagne*, that periodical judged Rousseau to be a Christian in morals only, and it went on to state that his reflections on miracles "might give him [the reader] no advantageous idea of that veneration for the sacred Writings our Author pretends to. . . . Mr. Rousseau's manner of Christianizing, if we may be allowed the term, is indeed very singular."[50]

The events following *Émile*'s condemnation pushed Rousseau into a rebellious attitude and caused his pages to bristle with himself and the violation of his rights. Constantly putting

himself forward, he seemed driven by an egregious and culpable vanity, and to the increasing number of the ill disposed,
exhibitionism offered the most satisfying explanation for what
now seemed to be his endless heterodoxies and misadventures.
With Rousseau it became almost obligatory to engage in *ad
hominem* criticism. According to the psychology of the ruling
passion, his vanity explained everything. His style was a cosmetic, his religion insolence, his politics conceit. And the spot-
light of controversy his highest good. As Rousseau made his
way across Europe toward a personal encounter with the
English people, the latter were still disposed to act the part of
protectors of persecuted intellect. But as Rousseau's physical
person entered London on January 13, 1766, his unattractive
personal history was already beginning to dominate the formation of his reputation. Eventually such matters as his really
quite mad conduct in England would destroy the majority's
admiration for Rousseau, and that which replaced admiration
was a gloomy portrait of at best a madman to be pitied, at
worst a scoundrel to be execrated.

We have thus far delayed any direct discussion of the *Contrat
social.* Although it was published in 1762, it was not until the
last, revolutionary decade of the eighteenth century that this
treatise received anything like significant recognition. The
notion of a revolutionary Rousseau did indeed emerge in the
1760s. It emerged, however, not from the precise theories of
the *Contrat social* but from the hectic accumulations of notoriety
and controversy which we have been outlining. As D. Mornet
succinctly puts it, "c'est à peine si l'on parle de ce livre redout-
able avant 1789."[51] Aware that Robespierre venerated Rousseau, historians and Rousseauists have often assumed that
Rousseau's most ambitious and succinct statement of political
theory must have been a fundamental cause of the Revolution
and a large factor in eighteenth-century attitudes toward Rousseau. On the contrary, the publication of the *Contrat social*
hardly ranked as a shot heard round the world. In England
both the *Monthly* and the *Critical* gave long summary-reviews of
Émile, but they ignored the fifth book's long abstract of the *Contrat.* And the work itself had to wait almost two years for an

English translation. The fact is that Rousseau's offenses never did take place in a civilized land of books and rational debate. They occurred, rather, in a frontier wilderness of European consciousness, a place where political and religious watchdogs stood ready to growl and snap at any too sharply critical intruder. Indeed, the first English notice of the *Contrat social* actually praised its politics as "[breathing] a free and liberal spirit," but it went on to direct most of its energies against the civil religion and especially the supposed unsuitability of Christianity as such a civil religion:

the meanest Christian must make a better patriot, and a much more social being, than the model of perfection which John James exhibits in his *Natural Man*, who runs wild and naked in the woods upon his hands and legs, eats acorns, shuns his species, only when the spirit of copulation moves him, [*sic*] and lives and dies among his brother-brutes.[52]

With Rousseau attacking his readers' religion as social convenience no less than as revealed truth, objective judgment had a meager chance indeed, and for Rousseau's quarrel with Europe, new metaphors began to suggest themselves. It was perhaps not quite the case that Rousseau was fighting the lonely fight for freedom of thought in Europe. Perhaps Europe was being asked to swallow whole the productions of a fantasy-monger, and, like the healthy organism that she was, Europe was having none of it. Perhaps Rousseau was not Socrates at all, and perhaps the body politic was simply rejecting a foreign and hostile malignancy.

IV

By the end of 1765, Rousseau had had enough of fleeing from one country to another. He thought first of going to Berlin under the personal protection of Frederick, but then (upon the urging of what remained of his French friends) he decided on England. His guide and host was to be David Hume, who as secretary to the British ambassador in Paris was about to return to England. Although he had never met Rousseau, Hume

chose to offer his services and to disregard the French intellectuals' warning that even *le bon David* could not sustain a friend-
ship with Rousseau.

The story of the falling out of Hume and Rousseau has been
told in detail. It is fully a half-century since Margaret Hill
Peoples gave us a very comprehensive chronology of events,
and more recently Lester Crocker has provided us with a succinct and thoroughly admirable account.[53] The root of the
quarrel lay in the sharp disparity of temperament between the
two men. A complicated web of misunderstanding developed
when Rousseau repeatedly thought he was appealing to Hume
for an explanation that the phlegmatic philosopher, seeing
neither the request nor its need, repeatedly failed to give.
Meanwhile, at the other end of the misunderstanding, Rousseau imagined that Hume only pretended not to understand
and kept silent only because he could not possibly justify himself. Hume may perhaps have been too inquisitive about Rousseau's personal affairs and less than candid in responding to
Rousseau's signs of resentment. He may also have felt somewhat guilty about certain mockeries of Rousseau (by Horace
Walpole) which he had countenanced in his presence. Nevertheless, Rousseau's accusations of calculated perfidy remain
false, outlandish, and paranoid. They are evidence of a disor-
dered mind, and the only valid complaint to be made against
Hume is that he did not sufficiently appreciate and pity this,
but instead reacted in a self-righteous dudgeon, hastily revealing Rousseau's enormities to those in Paris whom he knew to
be Rousseau's enemies.[54]

In the end, a Rousseau isolated in Derbyshire wrote to
Hume, breaking off all correspondence and denouncing him
for having cajoled him into England so that he might "have
him." Understandably surprised, Hume reacted intemper-
ately. Almost immediately he confessed in a letter to the Baron
d'Holbach that indeed he had been nursing a viper in his
bosom. Soon all of Paris knew about Rousseau's strange and
ungrateful conduct, and once the Paris *salons* knew this much,
it was only a matter of time before the whole affair became
public. When someone printed a letter of Rousseau's claiming

that Hume would not dare print the truth, the latter took it as a challenge and proceeded to demonstrate that he could indeed relate the entire incident. By October the *Exposé succinct de la querelle qui s'est élevée entre David Hume et J.-J. Rousseau* was out—a pamphlet containing a six-thousand word letter of Rousseau's which was as sublime in its style as it was demented in its conception of the writer's grievances.[55]

What went on between Rousseau and Hume was little more than a personal quarrel. But the disputants were two of the most famous men in Europe, men whose rupture was immediately of public interest. This was especially true in Paris where the first account of the quarrel àppeared in a French translation done under the direction of d'Alembert,[56] and where the disclosure of Rousseau's disgraceful conduct was very opportune for his numerous enemies.[57] For a decade the most bitter estrangement had separated Rousseau from such powerful pens as Diderot, Grimm, and Voltaire. Once Rousseau's injustice to Hume became public property, these literary arbiters of France acted as one might expect. They acted as if open season had been declared on Rousseau.

Immediately before Rousseau's quarrel with Hume, Voltaire, in the *Lettre au docteur J. J. Pansophe*,[58] had already mocked the Swiss moralist as a crazed votary of "sublime virtue," who, like everyone else in England, should establish a church, sure to do great work in making men there as stupid and ignorant as Rousseau's own beloved savages. But compared to what would follow, this was lighthearted banter, not to mention a lefthanded compliment to "virtuous" Rousseau. With public disclosure of the quarrel, criticism could now become much more serious and much more scabrous. Capitalizing on the falling out with Hume, Voltaire could now afford to be more pointed. He wrote an open letter to Hume, which he acknowledged, and notes to the letter, which he did not acknowledge.[59] In the letter, he characterized Rousseau as a man seditious, ungrateful, quarrelsome, vulgar, lewd, vain, and blasphemous. He even asserted that Rousseau wrote an incorrect French; and he concentrated his horror of Rousseau in this mythological genealogy: "Celui-là, certes, a eu raison qui a dit que Jean-Jacques descendait en droite ligne du barbet de Diogène accouplé avec une des couleuvres de la Discorde.''⁶⁰ Such open contempt was the order of the day. Grimm's *Correspondance littéraire* for September, 1766, printed the following:

Les plénipotentiaires médiateurs [for the civil discord in Geneva] viennent de deceler solennellment, et par écrit, que Jean-Jacques Rousseau n'est qu'un calomniateur. Cette declaration, jointe à celle de Monsieur Hume, est le juste châtiment d'un polisson qui est devenu un scélerat par un excès d'orgueil. Il est plus coupable que personne envers la philosophie; d'autres l'ont persécutée, mais il l'a profanée.⁶¹

While the *philosophes* believed Rousseau to be wicked, the English merely thought him mad. And if the affair with Hume had not sufficiently demonstrated this, the manner of Rousseau's subsequent flight from England most emphatically did. Sure that someone was about to seize him, Rousseau fled from his lodgings, ending up, on May 5, 1767, in Spalding, Lincolnshire. There he wrote the following extraordinary appeal to the Chancellor of England, which, like most of Rousseau's more imprudent missives, quickly found its way into the English press:

Arretté dans ces lieux par l'impossibilité eprouvée d'aller plus loin seul et sans danger, J'ai cru que le premier ministre des Loix devoit l'etre aussi de l'hospitalité publique et j'ose supplier de vouloir bien m'accorder à mes frais un guide autorisé, qui me conduise directement et sûrement au port de Douvre, où j'ai dessein de m'embarquer sans porter une pleinte contre personne.⁶²

And so England, long the distant spectator of Rousseau the eloquent writer, became the theater for the last and noisiest outburst of Rousseau the paranoid. Occurring in complete view of the public and at a time when Rousseau was frantic, the affair left the English with a sharp and intimate impression of Rousseau's madness. Even Boswell cooled in his enthusiasm. In his 1768 book on Corsica he wrote:

Rousseau was then [1764, when Boswell visited him at Motiers] living in romantick retirement, from whence, perhaps it had been better for him never to have descended. While he was at a distance, his singular eloquence filled our minds with high ideas of the wild philosopher. When he came into the walks of men we know alas! how much these ideas suffered.[63]

Since England knew that it had not played the part of persecuting Athens, the mantle of Socrates could not remain on the shoulders of Jean-Jacques. Another script would have to be written, and the *philosophes* stepped forward with the necessary characterization, insisting upon the egregious pride and misanthropy of this apostate from their ranks. In order to understand such startling and irrational conduct, however, most Englishmen had to reach beyond the boundaries of calculated wickedness. To them the only thing that seemed to explain the appearances was madness, and Rousseau's literary output began to be viewed in England somewhat as if it were a specimen of abnormal psychology, hardly a serious prescription for a new moral and political order: "Mr. Rousseau is indeed of little use: he may however amuse men of mere imagination, or such as like to contemplate the caprices of the human brain."[64]

In the conclusion to his account of the quarrel, Hume offered two possible explanations for Rousseau's conduct. If he was insincere in his accusations, he made them so that, puffing himself up as a decliner of royal favors (Hume had been urging Rousseau to accept a pension from George III), he might provoke a dispute and release himself from the annoying and demeaning obligations of gratitude. On the other hand, if Rousseau was indeed sincere, he must "imagine himself the sole important being in the universe . . . [and fancy] all mankind to be in a combination against him."[65] In either case Rousseau was guilty of "excessive pride," its deliberate nourisher or its delerious victim. Reenter the hackneyed but newly dramatized charges of vanity and "love of singularity."

There were many, though, who would not credit the *philosophes* in anything they said, people for whom the French intellectuals' quarrel with Rousseau was a point in his favor. These people were quick with explanations both for Rousseau's supposed love of singularity and for his indecorous conduct with

Hume. Singularity? Mediocre thinkers and writers thought
Rousseau willfully strange because they could not appreciate
his greatness, because, as Arthur Young wrote in 1769, "his
genius moved in a sphere superior to their own."[66] Rousseau's
emotional debacle with Hume? That was only another proof,
albeit unfortunate in its kind, of Rousseau's preternatural
sensitivity. As one eulogist put it, he was "cet homme extra-
ordinaire, qui fait la gloire de notre siècle, malgré les écarts où
son imagination, les vives emotions de son âme, et l'extrême
sensibilité de son coeur l'ont quelque fois jeté."[67]

As Rousseau returned to France from England, there remained to him an entire anticlimactic decade before he was to
die on July 2, 1778. During these years there is a pervasive
sense of all frenzy spent, a general stilling of the waters in both
the personal life and the public reputation. For the first three
years he lived in various parts of the French provinces, still
under penalty of arrest from the Parlement of Paris and for a
long time bearing the alias of "Renou." In 1770 he returned to
Paris where, aside from a brief period of reading the *Confessions*
in the literary *salons*, he lived very quietly, copying music,
botanizing, and writing still more autobiographical works.
Such life in retirement impressed many as a very appropriate
mental-asylum existence. To his devotees, however, it was just
another example of their philosopher's great virtue, his austere
simplicity of manners, and his renunciation of worldly honors.

A few months before he died, at the invitation of René de
Girardin, Rousseau moved into a small house on the grounds
of Ermenonville, just outside Paris. There Girardin had
planted an English garden adorned with monuments to Rousseau and other heroes of human progress. A cult was forming
around Rousseau, and when he died, it found in Ermenonville
a shrine ready to hand. For the reports of Rousseau's death
resemble nothing so much as hagiography. The following "last
words" of Rousseau are a lengthy eyewitness account, reproduced in Grimm's *Correspondance littéraire*, and from there translated to the pages of the *Monthly Review*, the *Gentleman's Magazine*, and the *London Magazine*. The latter even adorned its May

1779 issue with a frontispiece of Rousseau's tomb on L'Île des Peupliers in Ermenonville.

Ma chere femme, rendez-moi le service d' ouvrir les fenêtres . . . que j'aie le bonheur de voir encore une fois la verdure. . . . Comme elle est belle! Que ce jour est pur et serein! . . . O que la nature est grande! . . . Voyez le soleil dont il semble que l'aspect riant m'appele; voyez vous-même cette lumière immense: voilà Dieu, oui, Dieu lui-même qui m'ouvre son sein, et qui m'invite enfin à aller goûter cette paix éternelle et inaltérable que j'avais tant désirée[68]

As Rousseau would have wished it, the doctrinal letter of his cult was vague. Its spirit, however, might be inferred from the reliefs on his mausoleum: two doves for *La Nouvelle Héloïse*; a mother nursing her child for *Émile*; "children sacrificing on the altar of nature"; and "a lyre, with other symbols of poetry and music." The pre-Revolutionary cult of Rousseau was not political but aesthetic. What it saw Rousseau promulgating was not so much liberty, equality, and fraternity as the feeling heart, the simple life, and the familial bond.

A saint in the making, the late M. Rousseau was the same man whom Diderot immediately denounced as an "homme atroce," an ingrate, and "un artificieux scélérat, qui, pour donner quelque vraisemblance à ses injustes et cruelles imputations, se peindrait lui-même de couleurs odieuses."[69] The feelings provoked by Rousseau were religious at least in their intensity. He was a golden calf, one man's divinity and another man's abomination. What Diderot feared was the soon to be published revelations of the *Confessions*: anxious about his own reputation, he attacked Rousseau's personal character. To the more distant, however, Rousseau's history seemed unfortunate and frantic, but not deliberately wicked; and the English critics sharply censured Diderot (and others, such as Palissot and d'Alembert) for what they called slanders against the memory of Rousseau.[70]

It would appear that as the details of Rousseau's life receded in memory, the eloquence of his work was once again set free to work its magic on those who remained relatively untouched by personal bias. Meanwhile, an increasingly high value was beginning to be placed on sensibility. It is a somewhat cruel irony that only a decade after the persecution of Rousseau, a devout clergyman like James Beattie should praise him as a "moral writer of true genius." In what Beattie seems to have sensed as a required explanation, he pointed to Rousseau's heightened sensibility, an attribute with some liabilities but more assets: "Rousseau is, in my opinion, a great philosophical genius; but wild, irregular, and often self-contradictory . . . but of a heart too tender, and an imagination too lively to permit him to become a thorough-paced infidel."[71] The same note was struck at the *Monthly Review*. After stipulating the usual reservations about Rousseau's "self-applause," as well as his "judgment and reflecting powers," that periodical went on to conclude its portrait in a crescendo of praise for this man "whose heart was made to feel the *great*, the *good*, the *beautiful*, and the *affecting*, and whose vivid fancy gave them such forms as made others feel them also."[72] The "tender heart" and the "lively imagination"—these were again being seen not as Rousseau's problem but as his strength.

At his death, Rousseau was, in France, both a vessel of wrath and the center of a cult. To the more disinterested English, his reputation still hung in the balance. Knowledge of those actions that had been the object of denunciation certainly qualified admiration for the literary genius, but as former eyewitnesses of Rousseau's disturbed condition in 1766–1767, the English compassionately endeavored to understand it less as Rousseau's fault than as his involuntary fate. The *Universal Magazine*'s summation of the incongruities was typical: "one of the greatest and most distinguished characters that ever dignified human nature by the noblest conceptions, or rendered it pitiable by the most childish weaknesses."[73]

Although the English press discounted the personal attacks of Diderot, it was not at all certain that "a moral writer of true genius" was to be the last English word on Rousseau. It was only ten years since the man himself had departed from Dover very much in the style and very much with the explanations of a madman, and such erratic behavior was simply too recent and too notorious for his hosts to have entirely forgotten it. The posthumous publication of the *Confessions* would interdict any resurgent indulgence toward Rousseau as either writer or moralist. It would reinstate the personal perspective, and the French Revolution (for which Rousseau was supposed responsible and against which the English were soon to mobilize) very quickly turned this new English look at Rousseau into the most unqualified species of *ad hominem* invective. To the extent that Rousseau was to become an officially decreed hero of the Revolution, to just that extent he was to become an abomination to the counterrevolutionary island on the other side of the channel.

2

The Confessions *in*
English Politics

THE DEATH of Rousseau in 1778 by no means solidified his reputation. One very important and very sensational matter had not yet come to light. The first six books of the *Confessions* were not published until 1782, and the second six did not follow until seven years later, in 1789. Since previous disapproval of Rousseau had been fanned almost exclusively by the breath of personal obloquy, it was to be expected that Rousseau's public confiteors would give his critics a decided polemical advantage. The new Rousseau, youthful subject as well as middle-aged biographer, did not win much praise for his candor, goodness of heart, or psychological acumen. The almost unanimous reaction was a firm negative, and even many friendly to Rousseau expressed the wish that the *Confessions* had never been published.[1] Rousseau enthusiasts became Rousseau apologists.

The seemingly trivial and often tawdry experiences of a young vagabond radically altered the English image of Rousseau. An equally radical transformation would later be brought about by great historical events, or, more precisely, by the vagabond's presumed effect on these great historical events. The *Confessions* rescued from oblivion the early years of Rousseau's life and conferred upon them the dignity of history. Conversely, the men who would shortly be naming Jean-Jacques the father of the French Revolution would thereby add to the agenda of the Rousseau debate that massive upheaval of European society. Blamed or praised for the course of modern history, Rousseau became a touchstone of allegiance in world politics. In Pitt's England, he became an eponym for revolutionary mischief.

When, four years after Rousseau's death, the *Confessions* first appeared, they met with a very surprising reaction: almost universal disappointment. To explain such a response to the memoirs of this extraordinary man, one must remember that in 1782 only the first six books of the *Confessions* appeared, and that until 1789 the published memoirs ended with Rousseau as a thirty-year-old drifter almost a decade away from the first discourse. Voices praising these books as the "spring and source"[2] of the great man or as "a real and singular picture of the human mind"[3] were rare; most seemed to share the succinctly expressed judgment of the *Monthly Review*: "The Confessions end, where we wish they had begun, at his settlement in Paris."[4]

Unable to see beyond the superficialities of such a life, readers missed the point and wandered into random denunciation of such things as Mme de Warens' "street-walker"[5] morals or Rousseau's own residence in a moral "abyss."[6] The *Confessions* 1–6 offered a wealth of indecencies at which revulsion could forever rail: sexual deviance, cowardice, religious hypocrisy. But what made even these seem minor was the sheer fact of their self-advertisement, the ludicrous self-importance of such an undertaking:

a man whose vanity and presumption so imposed on his understanding, as to lead him to imagine that mankind would lend a ready ear to the most trifling, to the most dull, to the most impertinent, to the most disgusting relations, because they concerned ROUSSEAU! that they would examine every folly, and forgive every fault, because they were the follies and faults of the incomparable Author of *Emilius* and *Eloisa*.[7]

Rousseau's sense of his own importance now seemed to have overstepped the bounds of rationality as well as decorum.

Reviewing the *Rêveries du promeneur solitaire*, the editor of the *Monthly Review* could not resist the very unorthodox insertion of a bogus subtitle: "(. . . rather the Sublime Ravings)."[8]

The *Monthly*, which judged Rousseau's previous work favorably and even enthusiastically, chose to conclude its review of the *Confessions* with the following prediction:

Upon the whole, it is certain, that this publication will diminish considerably the high idea, which has been formed of M. Rousseau, and will perhaps lower him in the esteem of the Public more than he deserves to be.[9]

But the distaste that greeted the *Confessions* in 1782 was a reaction as ephemeral as it was superficial. Within less than a decade critics were daring to venture beyond the mask of personality. When in 1790, the newly found *Analytical Review* chided the critics for the "great contempt" shown toward the *Confessions*,[10] it voiced a complaint that was already becoming unnecessary. The critics seemed themselves ready to change their minds. They too were beginning to suspect that Rousseau's psychological disrobing was both a necessary and a courageous act—a contribution to the Socratic enterprise of self-knowledge. If the critics did not become excessive in their praise, they did at least qualify their disapproval. In 1782 the *Monthly Review* had been very severe on Rousseau. In 1790 it chose to conclude its review in a crescendo of praise:

Whatever little frailties there might be in his character, the writings for which he was so unjustly persecuted survive the malignant efforts of civil and ecclesiastical tyranny to suppress them, and will transmit to posterity, a lasting monument of the goodness of his heart, of his love of mankind, and of his zeal for virtue and the rights of his fellow creatures.[11]

The *Monthly* still felt that Rousseau "was often led away by strong passions, and wanted firmness of mind to regulate his conduct,"[12] but it could fully share the *Critical Review*'s belief in the utility of this picture of "a heart endued with the most exquisite sensibility, of a soul refined so delicately as to feel the highest pain or pleasure from circumstances which others would have scarcely noticed, or soon forgotten."[13]

Digging beneath the surface of one man's life, readers were discovering in the *Confessions* a rich and vital portrait of humanity. This trend, however, was short-lived. No sooner had the French Assembly decreed its honors to Rousseau than polemicists on the other side seized upon the *Confessions*, the *Rêveries*, and any other scraps of information useful in the *ad hominem* denunciation of revolution. Dwelling upon the most unedifying details, they proclaimed vanity and sensuality to be the keys to the diabolical kingdom that Rousseau had announced in his works, and which another upstart from Corsica was soon to bring to a bloody fruition. A partisan English public now regressed to the language, but seldom to the sincerity, of moral indignation.

The process by which Rousseau came to be honored by the French is neither as simple nor as direct as the usual assumptions about the *Contrat social*'s influence might suggest.[14] The National Convention's Committee on Public Instruction, although it yielded to no one in its praise of the *Contrat social*, explicitly questioned the general assumption of its great revolutionary influence. It pointed, instead, to the moral regeneration implicit in Rousseau's educational scheme according to Nature:

C'est en quelque sorte la Révolution qui nous a expliqué le *Contrat social*. Il fallait donc qu'un autre ouvrage nous amenât à la Révolution, nous élevât, nous instruisît, nous façonnât pour elle; et cet ouvrage, c'est *Émile*, le seul code d'éducation sanctionné par la Nature.[15]

The Revolutionaries were eager to honor what they accused the old order of persecuting, and so they set up "natural" Rousseau not as a pariah but as a martyred prophet of their own professed values:

honorez l'homme solitaire et champêtre qui vécut loin de la corruption des villes et loin du faux éclat du monde, pour mieux connaître, mieux sentir la nature et y ramener plus puissament ses semblables, honorez en lui le malheur . . . [*sic*] car il est douleureux et peutêtre inévitable que le génie et la vertu soient en butte à la calomnie, à la persécution des hommes, lors même qu'ils s'occupent des moyens de les rendre heureux, et Rousseau paya plus qu'un autre cette dette du génie et de la vertu.[16]

Although the eventful life bulked large in Rousseau's reputation, the Revolutionaries chose instead to adopt as a description of his most essential qualities the martrydom to be extracted from his quarrels with authority and the brilliant vision of beneficence to be found in his literary productions. A summary of the symbolic contingents accompanying the procession of Rousseau's ashes into the Pantheon shows how much the Revolutionary Rousseau was identical with the idol of the cultists.[17] Predictably there are a number of vague political representations: the National Convention; the people; the rights of man "qu'il réclama le premier"; and the Genevan Republic "qui a enfin vengé sa mémoire des outrages des aristocrates genevois." Then there are the less grandiose participants: mothers and children "qu'il reporta . . . entre les bras de la nature"; the mechanical arts in which he appreciated the dignity of man's labor; botany, "l'étude de la nature qui le consolait de l'injustice des hommes"; music "qu'il rendit . . . à son innocence primitive"; and Ermenonville and Montmorency, two pastoral asylums associated with his name. All these components of Rousseau's career possess one thing in common: a simplicity deemed to be synonymous with the natural. When the National Assembly of Geneva chose to erect a monument to their compatriot, it selected a simple column, surmounted by a bust and placed in the middle of an open field just outside the city walls. The reason for their rejection of anything more lavish seemed significant enough to be included in the public document: "Considérant . . . que plus ce monument sera simple, plus il se rapprochera des principes de J.-J. Rousseau."[18]

As enthusiasm for "simple" Rousseau thus became a predictable attitude of the revolutionary ethos, the execration of his memory turned into something like a sacred duty for the counterrevolutionary. The revolutionary contended that Rousseau was the father of his movement whom tyranny had persecuted for the prophetic espousal of his ideas. As this legend increasingly dominated the public imagination of Rousseau, the labels of counterrevolutionary and Rousseauist began to appear mutually exclusive. So successfully did the Revolution appropriate Rousseau that even its enemies recognized it as the holder of exclusive title to his name. But that counterrevolutionaries declined to dispute the affinity between Rousseau and the Revolution was a move deriving less perhaps from the merits of the case than from the obvious polemical advantages to be gained from the establishment of just such an affinity in the public imagination. For this bizarre memorialist of himself had surrendered a very powerful weapon to the political right, and it was one that the enemies of the Revolution did not hesitate to use. The *ad hominem* argument against Rousseau soon became a standard item in the arsenal of anti-Jacobin propaganda.

II

In England, for twenty-two years at war with France, the assault on Rousseau's reputation was fittingly led by the most influential of anti-Revolutionary writers, Edmund Burke. His *Reflections on the Revolution in France*, however, give Rousseau neither very much nor very vituperative attention. Burke's first and most extended phillipic devotes to Rousseau only a dozen or so lines in which Burke claims to have it from Hume that Rousseau deliberately used extreme situations and paradoxical expressions so as to excite wonder in his audience. It is only obliquely that Burke criticizes the mental lightweight from Geneva. His scorn is more pointedly directed at latter-day French disciples, legislators who would seek to found serious public policy on the performances of a literary mountebank. Burke even implies that the Revolution has been foisted upon Jean-Jacques: "I believe that were Rousseau alive and in one of his lucid intervals, he would be shocked at the practical frenzy of his scholars."[19] Being merely instrumental toward the censure of a Rousseau claque in the French legislature, Burke's portrait of Rousseau is as curt in its expression as it is sweeping in its judgments. The Rousseau to be found in the *Reflections* is a madman of consuming vanity, and it is a characterization the English polemicist does not take time either to explain or to defend. It is a self-evident truth, one that, for the moment at least, did not seem to require any further elaboration.

It was only shortly after the *Reflections* that the National Assembly of France publicly associated Rousseau with its own collective cause and policy. On December 21, 1790, it resolved that a statue commemorative of Rousseau be erected in order to illustrate the enlightened and virtuous policy of the new regime as well as to repair in some measure the contumely that the old order had heaped upon the person and works of "l'Homme de la Nature et de la Vérité."[20] To Edmund Burke this action of Revolutionary France was yet another revelation of the beast. It provoked him into writing a work that in its day was as popular and as influential as the *Reflections*, a work that now sent the English stock of Rousseau plummeting. Fully one-fifth of the *Letter to a Member of the National Assembly* (May 1791) is pure diatribe against the Revolution's newly honored hero. Condescension or comparatively mild rebuke are attitudes no longer appropriate to the French Assembly's "canon of holy writ."[21] The elements of the scoundrel remain the same: "vanity, possessed to a degree little short of madness,"[22] but the characterization is now more explicit than it is in the *Reflections*, the composition longer, and the delivery far more passionate.

In his *Letter to a Member of the National Assembly* Burke does not precisely say that Rousseau was responsible for the French Revolution, but it was largely as a result of this polemic that the assignment of such culpability soon became a commonplace in counter-Revolutionary propaganda. What Burke does do is to bring Rousseau forward as an officially decreed hero of the Revolution and thus as an example of the personal qualities the Revolution values: "Your Assembly, knowing how much more powerful example is found than precept, has chosen this man . . . for a model. To him they erect their first statue. From him they commence their series of honors and distinctions."[23] Burke perceives the Revolution's adulation of Rousseau not as historical effect but as an intended cause, the deliberate glorification of a human being who embodies the one quality deemed requisite for the citizens of the new society—vanity:

"Their great problem is, to find a substitute for all the principles which hitherto have been employed to regulate the will
and action."[24] They think they have found a solution in vanity.
Accordingly, for their guide and as their educational example,
they have chosen Rousseau "because in him that peculiar vice
which they wished to erect into ruling virtue was by far the
most conspicuous."[25] What Burke judges is not Rousseau the
political theorist but Rousseau the moralist. What interests him
is Rousseau's probable effect not on constitutional arrange-
ments but on the manners of society. He does not mention the
Contrat social.

Forseeing that a successful French Revolution would lead to
more than just a readjustment of governmental authority,
Burke feared that the baneful innovations of the Revolution
would have to extend themselves into the furthest reaches of
human experience, into values, attitudes, and manners. He
did not, therefore, consider a political pamphlet an inappro-
priate medium for the discussion of Julie and St. Preux's fictional passion. According to the rationale Burke very explicitly
puts forth in the *Letter,* such concrete representations can reveal
the shape of things to come. Models with which to judge the
new order, they can be turned into opportunities to discredit it:

the mode and the principles on which it [love] engages the sympathy
and strikes the imagination become of the utmost importance to the
morals and manners of every society. Your rulers were well aware of
this; and in their system of changing your manners to accomodate
them to their politics, they found nothing so convenient as Rousseau.
Through him they teach men to love after the fashion of philosophers:
. . . an unfashioned, indelicate, sour, gloomy, ferocious medley of
pedantry and lewdness,—of metaphysical speculations blended with
the coarsest sensuality. Such is the general morality of the passions to
be found in their famous philosopher, in his famous work of philosophic gallantry, the *Nouvelle Eloise.*[26]

From this description of Rousseau's novel, Burke goes on to
develop a rather far-fetched congruity between him and the
Revolution. According to Burke, Rousseau is a leveler as well

as a sensualist, a lustful underling who would have all the ser-
vants of the aristocracy seduce their female charges:

The rulers in the National Assembly are in good hopes that the
females of the first families in France may become an easy prey to
dancing-masters, fiddlers, pattern-drawers, friseurs, and valets-de-
chambre . . . By a law they have made these people their equals. By
adopting the sentiments of Rousseau they have made them your
rivals. In this manner these great legislators complete their plan of
leveling, and establish their rights of men on a sure foundation.[27]

Ostensibly Burke is judging *La Nouvelle Héloïse*. But, here as
elsewhere in these pages, the object as well as the manner of
Burke's accusation is intensely personal. What agitates Burke
in 1791 and what he belatedly finds reflected in Rousseau's
novel is the erotic misadventures of the author, so graphically
described in the *Confessions*. Particularly galling must have been
the former lackey's avowal that what he desired was not
common wenches but "demoiselles."[28]

Burke handles Rousseau in a very personal and inquisitorial
spirit. Declaring that the Revolutionaries' "standard figure of
perfection" is "a moralist, or he is nothing,"[29] he passes
quickly on to the evidence of Rousseau the man, his "practical
morality," as not only admissible but necessary for any just
estimation of his value. The private character of a man who
would teach others how to live, Burke contends, is always a
proper subject of inquiry. The way thus cleared for *ad hominem*
invective, he launches into his subject proper, the depraved
vanity of Jean-Jacques Rousseau, hero of the French Revolution:

We have had the great professor and founder of the *philosophy of vanity*
in England. As I had good opportunities of knowing his proceedings
almost from day to day, he left no doubt on my mind that he entertained no principle, either to influence his heart or to guide his understanding, but *vanity*. With this vice he was possessed to a degree little
short of madness. It is from this same deranged, eccentric vanity, that
this, the insane Socrates of the National Assembly, was impelled to
publish a mad confession of his mad faults, and to attempt a new sort
of glory from bringing hardily to light the most obscure and vulgar

vices which we know may sometimes be blended with eminent talents.[30]

Once Burke has uncovered Rousseau's ruling passion, he need address himself neither to the substance of Rousseau's thought nor to the quality and sincerity of his intentions. For it has now been discovered that all (of Rousseau at least) is vanity, everything else just a verbal cosmetic.

It is that new-invented virtue [vanity] which your masters canonize that led their moral hero constantly to exhaust the stores of his power-ful rhetoric in the expression of universal benevolence, whilst his heart was incapable of harboring one spark of common parental affec-tion. Benevolence to the whole species, and want of feeling for every individual with whom the professors come in contact, form the character of the new philosophy. . . . He melts with tenderness for those only who touch him by the remotest relation, and then, without one natural pang, casts away, as a sort of offal and excrement, the spawn of his disgustful amours, and sends his children to the hospital of foundlings. The bear loves, licks, and forms her young: but bears are not philosophers. Vanity, however, finds its account in reversing the train of our natural feelings. Thousands admire the sentimental writer; the affectionate father is hardly known in his parish.[31]

In Burke's hands, Rousseau the confessionalist is a weapon with which to destroy the credentials of Rousseau the moralist. By contrast Capel Lofft, a passionate English defender of Rousseau, urges his readers away from the life of Rousseau and toward his works, toward these "emanations of a sublime and benevolent mind . . . these charming pictures of innocent simplicity and rural happiness, opposed to the frivolity and pageantry of cities."[32] But even for such cultists as Lofft, the *Confessions* continued to be undeniably there—a constant em-barrassment "opprobriously dashed against [Rousseau's] Tomb by the revilers of his Memory."[33] It would not be long before such English admirers of Rousseau would begin to ap-pear even more willful than they were eccentric. For their admiration seemed to depend on a refusal to go beyond the enchanted circle of their idol's literary productions, and in anti-Jacobin England this was a stance that was to become increasingly more difficult to maintain. Burke's *Reflections* did indeed provoke a series of distinguished rebuttals—from Wollstonecraft, Paine, Mackintosh, Priestley—but the latter represent a set of liberal and radical opinion, atypical in 1791 and ever more marginal as France turned toward military adventures and Burke's perceptions began to establish themselves as dogma. The climate in England was not good for Rousseau's reputation: a preacher, calling Rousseau's influence "stupendous" and his message "sentimental profligacy," rejoiced along with the *Gentleman's Magazine* that Burke had unmasked such iniquity;[34] another popular monthly, the *Universal Magazine*, bludgeoned Rousseau with a piece of mindless hostility;[35] and even a would-be liberal like Jeffrey at the *Edinburgh* insisted that Rousseau's Revolutionary influence had been great and "unquestionably pernicious," Rousseau himself chargeable with the "highest presumption."[36]

The most direct descendent of Burke was the *Anti-Jacobin*, a ministry-subsidized organ of anti-Revolutionary malice which equalled its master in vehemence if not always in elegance. The periodical shovelled predictable contempt on the person of Rousseau:

[the better sort of readers saw in the *Confessions*] the characteristics of a selfish, depraved, and unprincipled profligate . . . [and beheld] in his public confessions of them a gross outrage of decency, an audacious contempt of morality, and a most impudent insult to the virtuous part of the community.[37]

The beautiful words of *La Nouvelle Héloïse* did not at all enthrall these defenders of Church and Crown. Beyond the scented loveliness they could see the furnace of lust, no less responsible for *Julie* than for the author's disgusting life: "his imagination transported him to the regions of enchantment, and all that the poets have told us of the isle of Paphos, came infinitely short of his delightful errors."[38] These comments occur in the *Anti-Jacobin's* review of a little catch-penny forgery published at Chambéry in 1786 and entitled *Mémoires de Mme de Warens suivis de ceux de Claude Anet*. It is, to say the least, peculiar that, twenty

years after the fact, a journal of public affairs should choose to
review such obscure trash, conveniently written and preserved
by the partners of Rousseau in a dubious ménage à trois, which
itself dates back to the 1730s. The incongruous appearance of
these patently spurious memoirs among kings and ministers is
very suggestive. It indicates the kind of personal calumny and
innuendo a counter-Revolutionary nation was prepared to use
against history's most egregious proto-Jacobin.

The politics of the *Anti-Jacobin* are extreme. A personally
based antipathy toward Rousseau, however, was scarcely an
attitude confined to the far right in England. Within ten years
of each other (1805–1813), two books appeared in which Rousseau played a large and unattractive role: Marmontel's *Mémoires*
and Grimm's *Correspondance littéraire*. In their devastatingly negative portraits of Rousseau, not one English reviewer found anything objectionable, except for perhaps too much indulgence
toward the scoundrel. There was a general English hunger for
ever more damning personal evidence against Rousseau, and
Marmontel and Grimm fed that hunger.

Marmontel's critique parallels that of Burke. Vanity was the
"poison" of Rousseau's life: the reason for his break with the
philosophes, for his paradoxes, and for his paranoia. The *Monthly
Review* knew a hatchet man when they saw one ("It is evident
. . . that he [Marmontel] felt a rooted dislike to Rousseau,
whom he holds up to reproach on every occasion")[39] but they
did not seem to consider the punishment unmerited. They ap-
provingly quoted Marmontel's entire character of Rousseau, a
neat exposition of monstrous vanity, soon reprinted for its
wider audience by the *Gentleman's Magazine*.[40] The once enthusiastic *Monthly* now judged Rousseau to be an "apostle of im-
morality."[41] Jeffrey at the *Edinburgh Review* was similarly disabused: "of the real character of Rousseau, we believe the
world is now fully informed. M. Marmontel represents it, we
think, with the utmost candour, and certainly in a light the
most unfavourable."[42]

Of all Rousseau's enemies the one from whom he expected
the worst was Baron Melchior Grimm. This quasi-official
chronicler of the Parisian literary scene was not, however, one

to lose his composure, least of all in print. As long as irony remained a weapon as effective as it was congenial, the *Correspondance littéraire* would contain no fulminations against Rousseau. Instead, Grimm would tap out perfunctory applause for Rousseau's great talents and then proceed to amuse himself with the humorless philosopher, directing at him a constant patter of worldly banter and refined innuendo. The following is an example of Grimm's habitual manner:

Jean-Jacques est venu deux cents ans trop tard; son vrai lot était celui de réformateur . . . au seizième siècle, il aurait fondé les pères Rousses ou Roussaviens, ou Jean-Jacquistes; mais, dans le nôtre, on ne fait point de prosélytes; et toute la prose brûlante n'engage pas l'oisif qui lit, à quitter le livre pour se mettre à la suite des prosateurs.[43]

In addition to ridiculing Rousseau as a wild-eyed fanatic, Grimm blithely refers to him as a misanthrope, a lunatic, a sensualist, an ingrate, a slanderer, a narcissist, a charlatan, and a sophist. Despite all this, the English reviewers were somehow taken in by the baron's gay, off-hand manner, judging him more appreciative of Rousseau than the latter perhaps deserved.[44] To the *Quarterly*, "Grimm appears to have always entertained a very high, not to say extravagant respect for the talents of this extraordinary man."[45] Similarly the *Edinburgh Review* wrote, "[Grimm] is very fair, and even very indulgent, to Jean-Jacques, through the whole of these speculations."[46] The English animus against Rosseau must have been very strong indeed, if observers could mistake Grimm's rapier thrusts for either praise or indulgence.

The loaded biographical approach to Rousseau was fast becoming the only approach. The *Confessions* had made clear the intimate if somewhat complicated connection between the fictional Julie and the real Mme de Houdetot, and even before that *La Nouvelle Héloïse* had usually been read as if it were cryptic autobiography. But now the same treatment began to be accorded even to Rousseau's more didactic and objective works. A typical analysis would go something like this: posing as a critic of society and government, Rousseau the fantasist had created various lands of heart's desire precisely because he had become so irrationally resentful of his fate in the real and necessary world of social distinctions; Rousseau was neither political theorist nor social critic; he was an escapist dreamer and indeed a very dangerous one:

he contracted a distempered sensibility, which forms the distinguishing feature of his character, and animates almost every page in his writings. He wrote from the heart; but from a heart excoriated by real or imputed wrongs, stung with a maddening sense of the depravity and sufferings of his species, and inflamed with an implacable indignation at the causes of these evils, as he viewed them, through his perturbed indignation, in the civil, social, and domestic institutions, the received opinions, and prevailing practices of mankind. Upon these accordingly he pours out, *in consuming fire*, the vials of his wrath; while he arrays in all the glowing hues of impassioned eloquence, romantic modes of being, dear indeed, and delightful to the fancy, but utterly incompatible with the real and unalterable condition of our nature.[47]

By 1813, it was widely accepted that Rousseau "followed an impulse originating exclusively in himself,"[48] and any ill-disposed critic could assassinate his character with the most exuberant confidence in the propriety of his methods. The *Monthly Review*, for example, began a discussion of Rousseau like this:

We will take the principal city at once,—we will march to his *heart* directly through his *Confessions*. The minor towns will fall all around us, for here is a clue to the conquest of the whole man. If we have but faith enough to believe that he tells the truth, the shameful truth, when relating his own actions, we see the cause of all his errors, of all his conduct, and all his writings: in two words, unmixed selfishness.[49]

The *Monthly*'s conclusion was pure Burke:

We can now easily unravel the cause of his aberrations from established principles in all his writings. The seductive enthusiasm of the Eloisa; the impractical theories of the Emilius; the still more absurd and visionary doctrines of his political writings; and the ungovernable anger of his controversial compositions, varied as they are in their effects, may, by patient application of the master-key here offered to our use, be all unlocked at their very source, and displayed to our sight, severally deriving themselves from their fountainhead of *self-ishness*.[50]

Assessing the place of Rousseau in history, the *Quarterly Review* likewise turned to personal criticism. To it, Rousseau's social criticism was nothing other than the injured pride of an adolescent vagrant:

After forsaking his religion and country, which imposed wholesome restraints upon his natural profligacy, he declared himself inimical to all human institutions, because while appearing under the character of a needy adventurer he had been treated with little hospitality.[51]

But along with many others, the *Quarterly Review* appreciated in Rousseau one positive quality that deserved to be saved from the general anathema. This was the power of sentiment:

Yet with all its defects, there are numerous passages in this celebrated work [*La Nouvelle Héloïse*] which astonish by their eloquence. Language perhaps never painted the conflicts of love in colours more animated and captivating than in the letter written by St. Preux when wandering among the rocks of Meilleray . . . yet with all his eccentricities, and all his failings, he is certainly one of the most fascinating writers that ever drew tears from a reader.[52]

If such a trenchant critic could thus praise Rousseau's sentimental talents, one might suspect that more receptive hearts would find in his work a power and grace of feeling redemptive of all possible faults. The very notion of sensibility, however, was itself undergoing a negative reappraisal, one not unconnected with the decline in Rousseau's reputation. For if Rousseau was one manifestation of the feeling heart, it was inevitable that the ideal of sensibility should itself begin to be suspect and hardly the cue for total forgiveness.

III

To appreciate the force with which the name of Rousseau suggested sensibility, one need only examine the public response to his minor posthumous works. By 1782, Du Peyrou, Rousseau's literary executor, had published a twelve-volume edition of the complete works, containing a good deal of previously unpublished material. When the *New Review* took notice of this edition, it chose to confine its remarks to the novelties, and, for all but one of them, it did scarcely more than note the fact of publication. The one exception was *Les Solitaires*, a novelistic sequel to *Émile* and "the only thing really worthy of Rousseau."[53] Fully two-thirds of the review records and celebrates the intensity of Emile's response to Sophia's infidelity. Here is definitely the sentimental Rousseau, or, as the critic puts it, "*verae voces pectore ab imo*, in English, the manners of nature, expressed in the strong language of the heart."[54]

In 1782 the *New Review* clearly meant these words in praise. But, particularly after the Revolution, not all those mentioning Rousseau's sensibility intended an accolade. Intimately associated with Rousseau's reputation, in its decline as in its ascendancy, was the value of sensibility, and even before the revolution, the *Confessions* seemed to justify, indeed to demand caution. The *Critical Review*, judging that Rousseau "was still [i.e., always] the slave of his feelings,"[55] explained the erratic behavior of his early years in the following way:

Endowed with a feeling heart, he seems for a time incapable of reason. Every action is the effect of momentary impression, and he is at once carried away by the sentiment, without being able to reflect on the tendency or the consequences of the action.[56]

The *Monthly Review* agreed, assigning to Rousseau "a mind wholly directed by the violent impulses of passion and feeling, unchecked by the cooler dictates of reason and philosophy."[57] And, within a few decades, even a fulsome admirer like Mme de Staël would admit that, although Rousseau possessed every other excellent quality of mind, he emphatically did not possess judgment.[58]

Ambivalence had, from the outset, consistently characterized the public response to Rousseau, and now, as Rousseau became increasingly identified with sensibility, the ambivalence toward him became one with the ambivalence of sensibility itself. As even a rather favorably disposed observer wrote in 1799,

The extreme and febrile sensibility which was the characteristic peculiarity of Rousseau . . . was, perhaps, a principal source of his greatness. It imparted a singular delicacy, freshness, and animation, to every page of his writings. His feelings, in whatever channel they flowed, rushed on with a restless impetuosity; but, in the end, they made a wreck of his understanding. His judgment was lost in the unremitting turbulence of his sensations; and, in some intervals of insanity, he exhibited the melancholy prospect of genius crumbling into ruins.[59]

It is an irony indicative of the ambivalent nature of sensibility that the *Confessions* indelibly fixed the image of sentimental Rousseau, first suggested by *La Nouvelle Héloïse*. For sentiment in *Julie* and sentiment in the *Confessions* are two quite different and even opposite things. The subject-author of the *Confessions* very often slips into sensuality. Julie and St. Preux, even when most ostensibly in the throes of lust, never descend from their high and noble plane. The two books are, as it were, an enactment of sensibility's ambiguity—Rousseau as "a motley association of the most elevated sentiments with the lowest propensities."[60] But with the *Confessions* so prominent in political polemic and so sharply fresh on the literary palate, English readers tended to look on the darker side of things. They would less often infer a good man from the fervent page than discredit the fervent page with the actions of a thoroughly bad type, a sentimental con man. The *Monthly Review* discovered a sensual center for every one of Rousseau's beautiful imaginings,[61] and even such an indefatigible defender of Rousseau's character and genius as the *Analytical Review* offered the following cautionary remarks about the *Confessions*:

his most enthusiastic admirers must allow that his imagination was sometimes rampant, and breaking loose from his judgment, sketched some alluring pictures, whose colouring was more natural, than chaste, yet over which, with the felicity of genius, he has thrown those voluptuous shades, that, by setting the fancy to work, prove a dangerous snare, when the hot blood dances in the veins.[62]

The author of these remarks is probably Mary Wollstonecraft. At any rate, the *Analytical*'s critique of Rousseauean sensibility coincides exactly with the anti-Rousseauean message of her *Vindication of the Rights of Women*.

Mary Wollstonecraft's immediate subject in the *Vindication* is Rousseau's system of female education, but it is clear that her characterization derives largely from the erotic adventures scattered throughout the *Confessions* which had thrust the "voluptuous reveries"[63] of *La Nouvelle Héloïse* into a rather more wanton light. A great admirer of *Émile*, Wollstonecraft was evidently quite disappointed when, finally arrived at the subject of women, Rousseau became the "philosopher of lasciviousness,"[64] gave up reason, and drifted into the prettinesses of the sentimental novel. As she saw it, the key to this falling-off was Rousseau's lustful nature: his "ruling appetite . . . disturbed the operation of reason."[65] So even the English left often felt forced to look upon the celebrated Rousseauean sensibility as something more candidly called sensuality, seemed forced to recognize the scandal of the *Confessions*, seemed driven into a biographical criticism that in the severity of its disapproval yielded little to the *Anti-Jacobin* right.

Lowering still further the English estimate of sensibility was their constant identification of it with the Rousseau whom the Jacobins so much admired. One of the *Anti-Jacobin*'s greatest delights seems to have been the uncovering of "senti-sensual nonsense"[66] in Rousseau. A celebrated cartoon of Gillray's lampoons the French Directory as professed worshippers of Justice, Philanthropy, and Sensibility.[67] The softest of the three Revolutionary goddesses is represented as a woman holding in her left hand a book inscribed "Rosseau" [*sic*] and in her right a dead bird over whom she weeps copious tears—while apparently unconcerned with the severed royal head under her heel. The figure illustrates lines, explicitly directed against Rousseauphiles and included in the "New Morality," George Canning's verse satire against the Revolution, which first appeared in the weekly *Anti-Jacobin*:

Mark her [Sweet Sensibility's] fair Votaries, prodigal of grief,
With cureless pangs, and woes that mock relief,
Droop in soft sorrow o'er a faded flow'r:—

But hear, unmov'd, of Loire's ensanguined flood,
Choak'd up with slain;—of Lyons drenched in blood;
Of crimes that blot the Age, the World with shame,
Foul crimes, but sicklied o'er with Freedom's name.[68]

One reason that sensibility went out of vogue was that revolutionary Rousseau had given it such a bad name. It was with no great originality that T. J. Hogg, Shelley's Tory friend, characterized some of the poet's pro-Revolutionary acquaintances as ''sentimental young butchers.''[69]

Eighteenth-century moralists readily discerned a family resemblance between the lewdness of young Rousseau and the Jacobin lust for blood. Both were forms of self-indulgence, a gratification of desire beyond the bounds of decency as well as those of social accomodation and compromise. As we have seen, Burke was no less insistent on the debauchery of the revolutionaries than he was on the destructiveness of the Revolution. Attempting to fathom the deeper causes of these deplorable events, he found what he thought was a hint in the Revolution's glorification of ''writers indulgent to the peculiarities of their own complexion.''[70]

When it first appeared in 1760, *La Nouvelle Héloïse* was hailed as a sentimental masterpiece. But by 1805, many had begun to doubt sentiment and its blessings—among them William Godwin, Shelley's future father-in-law and, for some time, his intellectual mentor. The subtitle of Godwin's *Fleetwood* makes clear the nature of his misgivings. Far from being a fount of benevolence, Godwin's ''new man of feeling'' is a brutal misanthrope placed in salient contrast with the old man of feeling, a benign patriarch once familiar with Rousseau and now presiding over a retired domestic situation modeled on the Clarens of *La Nouvelle Héloïse*. The theme of *Fleetwood* is sentiment and its ambiguity. Sentiment à la MacNeil (the patriarch) draws people together in affectionate cooperation; its model is the Clarens of Rousseau's imagination. Sentiment à la Fleetwood isolates; its model is the reality of Rousseau in the *Confessions*. Although the novel ends in conventional happiness, the endless tale of Fleetwood's brutality and madness suggests that his

species of sensibility was fast eclipsing the gentle domesticity of
the eighteenth century.

At the insistence of Fleetwood, MacNeil analyzes Rousseau.
He is conceded to have gone mad, to have been paranoid and
frantic "in a world of his own."[71] But, says MacNeil,

> he had such resources in his own mind! . . . his vein of enthusiasm
> was so sublime. . . . It was difficult to persuade myself that the person
> I saw at such times, was the same, as, at others was beset with such
> horrible visions.[72]

Godwin's representation of Rousseau in *Fleetwood* is anything
but simple. Rousseau is claimed as a spiritual ancestor both by
the title character and by MacNeil. While it is conceded that
Rousseau suffered from "horrible visions," it is likewise insisted that in *La Nouvelle Héloïse* he had developed a "vein of
[sublime] enthusiasm." There was, however, a line on the
English political terrain beyond which the heat and smoke of
counter-Revolution made it all but impossible to see moral
complexity as something applicable to the enemy. Beyond that
line in regard to the Revolution, most Englishmen were well
beyond it in regard to the scoundrel who was supposed to have
started it all. Having either forgotten or seen through the beauties of *La Nouvelle Héloïse*, they now judged Rousseau to have
been the disguised prototype of a new and very different man of
feeling—a brutal psychopath whose enthrallment within his
own nervous system was such that he could neither feel for nor
attend to anything else. They saw Rousseau and the Revolution as but two manifestations of the moral pattern Burke had
discovered within the events of his time: the show of tender and
equalizing sensibility; the reality of selfish and tyrannical
indulgence; the consequences of personal madness and public
carnage.

It is scarcely possible to overestimate the English influence
commanded by Edmund Burke for the several decades subsequent to his *Reflections on the Revolution in France*. Even for those
on the other end of the political spectrum, he remained the
interpreter of recent history who had to be answered, the prophet who had to be shown false. But if Burke on the Revolution

was a "canon of holy writ" for his compatriots, he was perhaps even more imposing on the more specific matter of Rousseau. In the *Letter to a Member of the National Assembly*, he had purported to reveal what kind of man Jean-Jacques really was, and with very few exceptions, his audience had taken what he said as gospel.

Included in Burke's diagnosis of Rousseau was the supposedly pathological fever of both his pen and his personality— that mine of individual expressiveness which, while it might look like precious sentiment, was really the genesis for catastrophes both private and public. The periods of Edmund Burke could not, however, fix so rigid and permanent a value on something as ambivalent as Rousseauean sentiment, and it was precisely along the fault of such ambivalence that Burke's xenophobic clarities about wild Rousseau would crack and shatter. For while Wordsworth and Coleridge did indeed model their Rousseau on the Burkean prescription, Byron and Shelley did not: in *Childe Harold* (canto 3, stanza 78), Rousseau is a lover of "ideal beauty," his passion fed by an "ethereal flame" and "teeming along his burning page"; and in Shelley's "Defence of Poetry," he is a "[poet] who had celebrated the dominion of love, planting as it were trophies in the human mind of that sublimest victory over sensuality and force." Although such casting of Rousseau into the Promethean mould is strikingly different from the sketches of Rousseau to be found in Burke and his followers, it is not very difficult to see how the one dialectically proceeds from the other. Quarreling with the National Assembly's commemorative statue, Edmund Burke knew in 1791 that its hero had his admirers in England as well. ("Thousands admire the sentimental writer.") He knew, too, that if one were successfully to tarnish Rousseau's name, one would have to prove counterfeit precisely that value of moral fervor with which many English still honored the newly proclaimed hero of the Revolution. He knew that he would have to confront what was ostensibly the fine moral sentiment of Rousseau and turn it into selfishness—disguised sensuality and hypocritical vanity. Such a polemical *volte-face* Burke did indeed accomplish, but once his hold on English opinion loosened somewhat, there was bound to be a revival of the Rousseau whom he had, as it were, devalued out of circulation: the Rousseau who was the "sentimental writer," the Rousseau whom some might think an authentic voice of nature speaking out against the divisive impostures of custom and caste, and so speaking out not from vanity but from love.

By reason of time, temperament, and political difference, Burke's influence lay much less heavily on Byron and Shelley than on Wordsworth or Coleridge. Seeing Burke as somewhat less than the perfection of political wisdom and not untouched by perversity, these second-generation romantics seem determined to say to their fathers in poetry, "Your evil, be that my good." For both Byron and Shelley recreated Rousseau in their own fire-bearing image. To them, Jean-Jacques became what he had always been to Hazlitt—not a detested *philosophe* but a fellow Promethean. The history of Rousseau's reputation among the English romantics is our next topic, and that history discloses (from yet one more point of view) just how necessary it is to make discriminations among the varieties of romanticism. For, on the matter of Rousseau, the party of Wordsworth and Coleridge was very different from that of Byron and Shelley. While the one came to rest in a Burkean withdrawal from all things revolutionary and Rousseauean, the other sought identity with a mantic Rousseau who was, for them, not so much the conventional persuasion toward caution and control as a new and inspiriting stimulus toward imitation, a lamp from which their own flames might gather more energy.

3

Rousseau and the Major English Romantics

In 1809 a patriotic William Wordsworth was quite certain that the agents of French cultural imperialism would not be solid enough to succeed on the Iberian Peninsula:

Nor has the pestilential philosophism of France made any progress in Spain. No flight of infidel harpies has alighted upon their ground. A Spanish understanding is a hold too strong to give way to the meagre tactics of the "Système de la Nature"; or to the pellets of logic which Condillac has cast in the foundry of national vanity, and tosses about at hap-hazard—self-persuaded that he is proceeding according to art. The Spaniards are a people with imagination: and the paradoxical reveries of Rousseau, and the flippancies of Voltaire, are plants which will not naturalise in the country of Calderon and Cervantes.[1]

Behind the blanket of contempt thus dropped on the company of Voltaire, Rousseau, Condillac, and Holbach is the spiritual progress traced in the *Prelude* of 1805. In that "growth of a poet's mind," the route had been anything but direct from the boy on the cliffs of Winander to the visionary in retrospect whom we follow up Snowden. While it may have been the goal of the *Prelude* to bound day to day in natural piety, it was not its method. The poem is, on the contrary, a less than flowing record of the many discontinuities that threatened but never quite shattered the imaginative wholeness of a young man who, making no vows, nonetheless had vows made for him, sacraments of identity which bound him to just those particularities of the English scene in whose presence he had become who he was. As unearthed by the *Prelude*, the hiding places of Wordsworth's power revealed themselves as insistently English, and as a corollary to this discovery, French "philosophism" became for Wordsworth an ever more superficial rationalism, begun in vanity and completed in flippancy. William Godwin's *Enquiry Concerning Political Justice* (1793) is neither French nor flippant, but as an extreme of affection denied and reasoning exalted—what William Hazlitt called an "Arctic Circle . . . where the understanding is no longer warmed by the affections"[2]—the book brought to a crisis that William Wordsworth who, pushing hard for precise answers and neat formulas, nonetheless could not become what he eventually took a *philosophe* to be: a man living in constant and affected denial of his own imaginative being. The "Convention of Cintra" uses language as strong as "pestilential philosophism" because it is written by a poet who, once infected, is now recovered, a poet who entitled the two penultimate books of his autobiographical epic "Imagination and Taste, How Impaired and Restored." What the "infidel harpies" of the Enlightenment had almost succeeded in withholding from this Englishman was imaginative nourishment.

Wordsworth's escape from the associated snares of abstract theorizing and uprooting political action describes a passage not so much from reason to feeling as from abstraction to particularity, from the universal but brittle maxims of the Enlightenment to the solidly insular convictions of an English poet, felt in the blood and along the heart. In his unpublished "Letter to the Bishop of Llandaff" (1793) a "republican" Wordsworth had used "philosopher" as a frequent and honorific title, had defended the revolution, and had quoted Rousseau.[3] But, by the time he was writing on the Convention of Cintra, Wordsworth had discovered himself to be as English as he expected the Spanish to be Spaniard. Although tempted, his native stock had not succumbed to the attractions of French sophistry, a commonplace example of which was the newfangled paradoxes

of Rousseau—an established cliché of English criticism, canonized by Johnson and Burke and now cast into the inflexibility of
a passion that was, for Wordsworth, more than simply personal
or political. It was poetic, the pride and strength of a "people
with imagination."

Wordsworth turns both the Enlightenment and the French
Revolution into episodes in his own spiritual development.
Thus enmeshed within the egotistical sublime, they are less
realities of public record than counters for personal history—
the one for "that false reasoning power / By which we multiply
distinctions," the other for the demoralizing consequences
attendant upon the unqualified application of that power to
human affairs.[4] Since conservative English opinion and the
twenty-two year old republican agreed on the close association
between Rousseau and revolution, it was possible for Rousseau
to become for the older Wordsworth a figure little read but
hugely significant. He was an ideological wild oat. To know
him as a *philosophe* was to know what was radically wrong with
him, and that was all an English poet needed to know.

The meager explicit notice Wordsworth takes of Rousseau
has not prevented later readers from seeing fundamental similarities and even suspecting a direct influence from one nature
loving egotist to the other.[5] The available record, however,
adds up to what Jacques Voisine characterizes as a virtual
vacuum, a "*surprenant mutisme a l'égard de Rousseau.*"[6] Although
the *Confessions* occupied a place in Wordsworth's library,[7] none
of his scanty references to Rousseau mentions either the man of
feeling or the autobiographer. On the contrary, these references
are, without exception, to the *philosophe*, to one of that intellectual company charged with collective responsibility for the
French Revolution by all shades of English opinion.

Such diminishing of Rousseau by association accounts for
the figure to be found in the writings of Wordsworth young and
Wordsworth old: the abstract political theorist so diligently
quoted in his "Letter to the Bishop of Llandaff" and the 1809
stereotype in which Rousseau and Voltaire are unlike writers
yoked together by political invective. It accounts also for the
hardly conservative but sufficiently bigoted William Blake—for

his depiction of Voltaire and Rousseau as the twin beacons of the Revolution, and for his "Mock on Mock on Voltaire Rousseau," a poem whose compressed dialectical progress toward a visionary Israel begins with the most conventional recreation of Rousseau not in the image and likeness of Émile or St. Preux but in that of the scoffing Voltaire.[8] Indeed, of the fourteen Rousseau entries to be found in the *Blake Concordance*, not a single one allows Jean-Jacques to stand free of Voltaire.[9] It is as if the prophetic wrath of Blake were directed against some hyphenated chimera always named Voltaire-Rousseau and usually accompanied by a veritable Babel of Enlightenment heroes and precursors—Gibbon, Hume, Bacon, Newton, and Locke. When Blake featured Rousseau in the address to the "deists" which inaugurates the third chapter of his *Jerusalem*, he was relegating him to the party of Urizen and natural religion, the party of the Enlightenment.[10]

Tagging Rousseau a *philosophe*, both Blake and Wordsworth impoverished his identity into something that, for their quite distinct reasons, they could have the pleasure of hating without qualification. In Wordsworth, such an attitude inhibited not only a possible chain of influence but perhaps also the generous acknowledgment of the manifest similarities discovered by later critics. This selective paucity of Wordsworthian allusion to Rousseau is a function of the tunnel vision of the English during the revolutionary period, an insular optics that, seeing Rousseau plain as a *philosophe*, either elided the man of feeling or brutalized him into a psychopath whose every word and deed epitomized just that kind of self-indulgence to be expected when the universalizing reason of Burke's abhorrence presumed to set the affective life free from the bonds of place and circumstance. As a Hazlitt, not unsympathetic to the Enlightenment, wrote about Godwin, "It was to be feared that the proud Temple of Reason, which at a distance and in stately supposition shone like the palaces of the New Jerusalem, might (when placed on actual ground) be broken up into the sordid styes of sensuality, and the petty huckster's shops of self-interest!"[11]

Insofar as it acknowledged a Rousseau different from the

other *philosophes*, patriotic England saw him not as opposed to their airy doctrines but as putting them into practice, driving them into the denouements of flesh and blood. In the political development of Samuel Taylor Coleridge, one may clearly see this tactic of brutalization, this reduction of Rousseauean sentiment into an unbridled self-indulgence deemed to be the incarnation of French ideas.

In the *Friend* of 1809, Coleridge had already arrived at what would remain his final opinion of Rousseau. In it he characterizes the "Continental Genius" not only as a skeptic set morally adrift from tradition but also as a slave to his "bodily temperament":

in the inauspicious Spirit of his Age and Birthplace, Rousseau had slipped the Cable of his Faith, and steered by the Compass of unaided Reason, ignorant of the hidden Currents that were bearing him out of his Course, and too proud to consult the faithful Charts prized and held sacred by his Forefathers. But the strange influences of his bodily temperament on his understanding; his constitutional Melancholy pampered into a morbid excess by solitude; . . . these, or at least the predisposition to them, existed in the ground-work of his Nature: they were parts of Rousseau himself.[12]

But the once enthusiastic advocate of pantisocracy had not always looked so reductively down on Rousseau. In a public lecture delivered on May 29, 1795, he had mentioned Rousseau's "heart" in terms little less than reverential. According to the young Coleridge, the "Miracle" of Christ's teaching had "convinced the doubting mind of Rosseau [*sic*], whose reasonings would not suffer him to believe the miracles of Jesus, but whose heart had too much of man, too little of Atheist in it, not to feel and profess, that the God of Love was in him, that the Spirit of the Most High dwelt upon him."[13] And in another youthful effort to unite Christianity with sensibility, Coleridge did not restrict himself to the heart that has reasons of its own. He pushed on to the social gospel, bringing his denunciation of wealth and inequality to a heated Biblical peroration only after he had first analyzed the Mammon of Iniquity according to the arguments of Godwin and Rousseau.[14] What set Rousseau somewhat apart, however, was less any social and economic theory, the egalitarian outlines of which he was perceived to share with other philosophers, than the man's unique moral fervor both on the page and in his life. Like his Unitarian Jesus, the Rousseau of Coleridge *aetatis 23* was a man of the heart, bearing witness to love and exposing the impostures of wealth and power. As Coleridge breathlessly put it to a radical rather less moved to such millenia-skipping assimilations: "But you cannot be a Patriot [i.e., a humanitarian] unless you are a Christian!—Yes! Thelwell! the disciples of Lord Shaftesbury and Rosseau, as well as of Jesus."[15]

As an earnest of things to come, one may note the transformation that Coleridge's lecture has undergone when it next appears as a sermon, delivered in Nottingham's High Pavement Chapel only eight months afterwards, on January 31, 1796:

[the miracles of Jesus] forced a dubious ray of Faith into the mind of Rosseau, whose reasonings led him to disbelieve the miracles of Jesus, but whose heart forced him to retire from the contemplation of Christ's character with the full conviction that the God of Love was in him, that the spirit of the most High dwelt upon him.[16]

The ray of faith in the *philosophe* is now "dubious," and gone also is the Rousseau who was so much the feeling man and so little the cold atheist. Behind such anxiously orthodox changes, there is not so much the lapse of eight months as the special audience of a sermon, but since the direction of Coleridge's thought was to become ever more explicitly religious, these changes may be seen as looking forward to the way Coleridge's position was to become fixed against so notorious a freethinker as Jean-Jacques Rousseau. The Swiss philosopher was definitely not on the side of the angels.

By November 1796, Coleridge was professing that he did "not particularly admire Rousseau."[17] By January 1800, he was mocking him, referring to the "ranting sentimental correspondence" of Charles Lloyd as something done "a la Rousseau."[18] Thereafter, there are only a few mentions of Rousseau in the voluminous correspondence of Coleridge, all of them both slight and slighting. In addition, the encyclopedic *Notebooks* are almost entirely silent about Rousseau, there being but one very brief reference to the "sophistry" of his unrealistic "Plan of Education."[19] Given the intellectual range of Coleridge's letters and notebooks, a suspicion *ex silentio* seems permissible: Coleridge neglected Rousseau not so much despite the latter's continental reputation as because of it. He would know all he needed to know about Rousseau once he knew that he was a *philosophe*, pursuing abstract reason with an eloquent obsessiveness impracticable in act but disastrous in consequence. That Coleridge's generic classification of Rousseau is identical with Wordsworth and Blake's bespeaks a community of prejudice so binding that it could be made to account for qualities in Rousseau apparently alien from the man of reason but really (so Coleridge and Burke would have it) indicative of just those failings proper to the type. For Coleridge was not Wordsworth. He could not stop at seeing Rousseau as a *philosophe* and then close the book on him. He had to find a place in his system for this philosophical exotic. To make his own sense out of Rousseau, he had to construe the celebrated sentiment not as a value counter to "our enlightened age," but as a consequence of it—what Burke had so aptly characterized as a mixture of profligacy and madness. The older Coleridge does not so much attend to the "thisness" of Rousseau as classify him and make the appropriate deductions. He gives every indication that he ignores the lush and hectic exfoliations of Rousseau only because he has already made up his mind that they too are to be traced back to that one dessicated root from which have sprung up all the other, more unambiguous, branches on the philosophic family tree. To Coleridge, Rousseauean sentiment soon ceased to appear Christlike. It became, instead, just that kind of vicious and heedless madness to be expected of a *philosophe*.

Coleridge's only published appraisals of Rousseau offer further evidence for what I would argue to be his defensive reaction against a Rousseau whom he praised in his youth and whose possible affinities with himself he needed to put behind

him as the offspring of "France . . . my Babylon, the Mother of
Whoredoms in Morality, Philosophy, Taste."[20] They both
appear in the *Friend* of 1809. One characterizes the *Contrat social*
as a treatise that would seek to lay the foundations for a theory
of government "exclusively in the pure reason."[21] The other is
a double-barreled comparison between, on the one hand, Erasmus and Luther—"the two Purifiers of revealed Religion"—
and, on the other, Voltaire and Rousseau—"the two modern
conspirators against its authority, who are still the Alpha and
Omega of Continental Genius." Although we once again find
the almost obligatory yoking with Voltaire, the imagination of
Coleridge is not, in this instance, one that has given the scoffer
the lead position and made Rousseau trot behind in traces of
exclusively Voltairean pressure. For while the comparison
between Erasmus and Voltaire is flimsily founded upon wit,
apologetically advanced and quickly dispatched, that between
Rousseau and Luther is extended into a diagnosis of the latter
which, for all its ritual obeisances to the first Protestant, nonetheless traces his salutary influence to the same delusory
megalomania for which Rousseau had become a byword. According to Coleridge, both Luther and Rousseau "referred all
things to his own Ideal." But for the believing times in which
he had lived, Luther would have ended up like Rousseau. He
"would have held himself for a Man of Genius and original
Power," his ideals would have shriveled into selfhood, and his
writings would have become engines of satanic destructiveness.
According to the epigraph Coleridge added to the 1818 version
of the essay, it was only Jehovah who had saved Luther from
himself:

[it behooves] us to consider, in how many instances the peccant
humour native to the man has been wrought upon by the faithful
study of that only faultless Model [i.e., the Bible], and corrected into
an unsinning, or at least a venial, Predominance in the Writer or
Preacher. Yea, that not seldom the Infirmity of a zealous Soldier in
the Warfare of Christ has been made the very mould and ground-
work of that man's peculiar gifts and virtues. Grateful too we should
be, that the very Faults of famous Men have been fitted to the age, on
which they were to act: and that thus the folly of man has proved the

wisdom of God, and been made the instrument of his mercy to mankind.[22]

Having no such divine savior, Rousseau had become not a prophet but a secular madman, "crazy ROUSSEAU, the Dreamer of love-sick Tales, and the Spinner of speculative Cobwebs; shy of light as the Mole, but as quick-eared too for every whisper of the public opinion; the Teacher of stoic *Pride* in his Principles, yet the Victim of morbid *Vanity* in his Feelings and Conduct!" Although all of Coleridge's remarks on Luther are a plagiarism,[23] the comparisons with Voltaire and Rousseau are his own, and if we in turn compare the comparisons, we may detect two complementary undercurrents, the latent disapproval of Luther being one with an even more submerged admiration for Rousseau. For while Coleridge emphatically asserts that the detested Voltaire could never have become an Erasmus, he does quite the opposite for the "better hearted" Rousseau. He insists that with Rousseau and Luther there is a "resemblance in the Men themselves, . . . [a] similarity in their *radical* natures." [Coleridge's emphasis]

The following hypothesis about a Luther displaced into the eighteenth century is the reality of Rousseau as Coleridge perceived it:

His impetuous temperament, his deep-working mind, his busy and vivid Imagination—would they not have been a *trouble* to him in a World, where nothing was to be altered, where nothing was to obey his Power, to cease to be that, which it had been, in order to realize his pre-conceptions of what ought to be? His Sensibility, which found Objects for itself, and shadows of human suffering in the harmless Brute, and even the Flowers which he trod upon—might it not naturally, in an unspiritualized Age, have wept and trembled, and dissolved over scenes of earthly Passion, and the struggles of Love with Duty? His Piety, that so easily passed into Rage, would it not have found in the inequalities of Mankind, in the oppressions of Governments, and the miseries of the governed, an entire instead of a divided Object? And might not a perfect Consitution, a Government of pure Reason, a renovation of the social Contract, have easily supplied the place of the reign of Christ in the new Jerusalem, of the restoration of the visible Church, and the Union of all Men by one

Faith in one Charity? Henceforth then, we will conceive his Reason
employed in building up anew the Edifice of *earthly* Society, and his
Imagination as pledging itself for the possible realization of the
Structure. We will lose the great Reformer, who was born in an Age
which needed him, in the Philosopher of Geneva, who was doomed to
misapply his Energies to materials the properties of which he misun-
derstood, and happy only that he did not live to witness the direful
effects of his System.

Thus obliquely critical of Luther, the passage is likewise
obliquely respectful of Rousseau. It locates the source of "his
serious and vehement eloquence . . . [his] elevated tone of
moral feeling" in a personality identical with that of the German "Son of Thunder" which, but for skepticism, might have
had the same renovating effect as the "Christian Hercules, the
heroic Cleanser of the Augean Stable of Apostacy."

Behind Coleridge's constant tirades against the licentious
minds and manners of the French, there thus emerges hints of
a more ambivalent attitude toward "crazy Rousseau"—a not
unadmiring demonization, a sensitivity to the seemingly raw
and unleashed energy of Rousseau's personality. But if the
Rousseau of the older and more conservative Coleridge is a
demonic force, he is one less to be revered than to be contained
and feared. To the disciple of Burke, recent history was but one
continuing demonstration that the eloquent Rousseau had
brought not airs from Heaven but blasts from Hell, had been
not the servant of the ideal but the slave of his own passionate
nature. And from such a demon Coleridge springs back with
repulsion. He springs back not only into a broad and rigidly
conceived critique but also into a somewhat uncharacteristic
mockery, both of them a defensive reaction to the seductiveness
he himself had experienced: "Experience has proved, that the
great danger of [Rousseau's] System consists in the peculiar
fascination, it is calculated to exert on noble and imaginative
Spirits; on all those, who in the amiable intoxication of youthful Benevolence, are apt to mistake their own best Virtues and
choicest Powers for the average qualities and Attributes of the
human Character." Faced with a demonic Rousseau, Coleridge seems to act out the concluding exhortation of his "Kubla

Khan'': "Beware! Beware! / His flashing eyes, his floating hair / Weave a circle round him thrice / And close your eyes with holy dread.''

Enlisting paradox into his armies of psychic defense, the increasingly orthodox Coleridge uncovers a man of reason at the source of prophetic eloquence gone both wild and secular. For if Coleridge sees Rousseau as peculiarly eruptive, he also sees the permissive cause of this special talent for destruction as no different from that behind the other *philosophes*. Rousseau too had "slipped the Cable of His Faith and steered by the Compass of unaided Reason." To Coleridge this genealogy of destructiveness seems clearest in what he understood to be Rousseau's political philosophy. Explicitly basing himself on the Burkean principle of expediency, Coleridge first assumes that the *Contrat social* best and most fully represents the principle of the French Revolution and then defines that principle as "the grounds of government, laid exclusively in the pure reason." Apparently ignorant of Rousseau's own efforts to think expediently about such real places as Geneva and Poland, Coleridge accuses him of constructing a political "geometry" that disregards how the particularities of time and place modify the concrete application of principle. To the extent that this "metapolitical" Rousseau never went "beyond the magic Circle of the pure Reason, and [into] the Sphere of the Understanding and the Prudent," his very idealism must be seen as an encouragement to the French people's progressively more brutal and self-serving embodiments of the *volonté générale*. Rousseau's theory may have been a "thing of air," but its results had proven to be very tangible indeed:

With a wretched *parrotry* they [the Constituent Legislators of France] wrote and harangued without ceasing of the *Volonté générale*—the inalienable sovereignty of the People: and by these high-sounding phrases led on the vain, ignorant, and intoxicated Populace to wild excesses and wilder expectations, which entailing on them the bitterness of disappointment, cleared the way for military Despotism, for the satanic Government of Horror under the Jacobins, and of Terror under the Corsican . . . [in whom] . . . MIGHT becomes RIGHT, and . . . HIS Cause and the Cause of God . . . one and the same. Excellent Postulate for a Choleric and self-willed Tyrant!

Referring his readers to Wordsworth's recently published tract on the Convention of Cintra, Coleridge fights the same battle for particularity against abstraction:

A Constitution equally suited to China and America, or to Russia and Great Britain, must surely be equally unfit for both, and deserve as little respect in political, as a Quack's panacaea in medical, Practice.

[Rousseau's] universal Principles, as far as they are Principles and universal, necessarily suppose uniform and perfect Subjects, which are to be found in the *Ideas* of pure Geometry and (I trust) in the *Realites* of Heaven, but never, never, in the Creatures of Flesh and Blood.

What recent history seemed to show was just how fleshy and bloody subjects could become when guided by a theory that supposedly took no cognizance of them except as disembodied intellects. Committed to this Burkean interpretation of recent events, Coleridge was moved to see Rousseau's manifest passion not as a contrast to the absentee rationalism of the Enlightenment but as its licentious consequence—the personal analogue and earnest of just those revolutionary excesses that were understood to have followed in the wake of Rousseau's theorizing. For Coleridge, the flights of reason had precipitated both man and nation into the pits of raw appetite and crazed delusion. Both had turned out anarchic the closer they came back to the particularities of home and self.

Given Coleridge's paucity of specific reference to Rousseau, it is perhaps unwise to make too much of but two essays, one mostly a character of Luther plagiarized from a German source, the other a rather glib dismissal of what Coleridge took to be the rationalist limitations of the *Contrat social*. It is, however, anomalous that Coleridge should neglect a man whom he himself characterizes as either the alpha or the omega of continental genius. The anomaly begs for an explanation. It suggests that Coleridge hardly ever talks about a specific Rousseau simply because he is always inveighing against the type to which he supposes the man to belong. An isolated character difficult to find in Coleridge's later writing, Rousseau nonetheless remains an implicit target of all those broadsides Coleridge never tired of launching against the entire alphabet of Jacobinism. For him, as for Burke before him, Rousseau is the proto-Jacobin, and his two essays in the *Friend* only seem to be his last public statements on Rousseau. For their picture of an egotist, philosophically abstracted, personally licentious, and demonically destructive, tallies perfectly with Coleridge's many subsequent jeremiads against the French Antichrist. In analyses like the following in *The Statesman's Manual*, Rousseau is never mentioned but always present:

> though the growing alienation and self-sufficiency of the understanding was perceptible at an earlier period, yet it seems to have been about the middle of the last century, under the influence of Voltaire, D'Alembert, Diderot, say generally of the so-called Encyclopedists, and alas!—of their crowned proselytes and disciples, Frederick, Joseph, and Catharine, that the Human Understanding, and this too in its narrowest form, was tempted to throw off all show of reverence to the spiritual and even to the moral powers and impulses of the soul; and usurping the name of reason openly joined the banners of Antichrist, at once the pander and the prostitute of sensuality, and whether in the cabinet, laboratory, the dissecting room, or the brothel, alike busy in the schemes of vice and irreligion.. . . . Prurient, bustling, and revolutionary, this French wisdom has never more than grazed the surfaces of knowledge. . . . As the process, such the result! a heartless frivolity alternating with a sentimentality as heartless—an ignorant contempt of antiquity—a neglect of moral self-discipline—a deadening of the religious sense, even in the less reflecting forms of natural piety—a scornful reprobation of all consolations and secret refreshings from above—and as the caput mortuum of human nature evaporated, a French nature of rapacity, levity, ferocity, and presumption.[24]

In this character of the entire French nation, rationalism and vice are the satanic complements of each other. As such, this character is identical with what an embattled England had attributed to Rousseau ever since Burke wrote his *Letter to a Member of the National Assembly* in 1791. That being the case, it is perhaps insufficient to say that Rousseau is an implicit subject of this xenophobic portrait; it may be more accurate (albeit unprovable) to say that notorious Rousseau is its unconscious model.

But whatever part the image of Rousseau may have had in the genesis and reinforcement of Coleridge's anti-Gallicism, it remains indisputable that he shared his xenophobia with Wordsworth and Blake and that he did so on the same basis of an assumed identification between France and an Enlightenment supposedly given over to lifeless generalization. Caught in the web of this national prejudice, these poets of the particular were not nearly particular enough about Rousseau. Professed enemies of pallid generalization, they nonetheless said very little specific to Jean-Jacques, and what they did say never went counter to the conventional English wisdom according to which he was yet another specimen of the genus *philosophe*. If, as Spinoza says, every determination is a negation, then such a patriotic insistence that Rousseau be a *philosophe* must be seen to negate much of what subsequent generations have found not only most interesting in Rousseau but also most contributory to the French Revolution and most cognate with English romanticism. In the end, then, the attitude of these great English poets toward Rousseau must be characterized as one of intellectual neglect and even repression. The politically heated times in which they came to personal and poetic maturity had, as it were, clamped an embargo on their minds, and they chose not to recognize what Jean-Jacques Rousseau most assuredly was within the confederation of French letters: a very independent principality.

Out of the rhetorical commonplaces of their time and country, Wordsworth and Coleridge spin slender and infrequent filaments of commentary on a Rousseau neither unique in station nor dense with complexity. But as conventional as the mite of attention they pay to Rousseau may be, it is not without its instructiveness. It underscores a lack of interest in the subject —a gap in attentiveness whose ultimate origin is the aggressively excluding certainties of political dogma. Wordsworth and Coleridge manifestly did not attend to the ''thisness'' of

Rousseau, and they did not attend to it because they thought this admittedly seminal figure of the age completely defined by the generic classification of *philosophe*, which Edmund Burke had so emphatically stamped on him more than two decades before at the commencement of Franco-English hostilities.

II

The repression of the man of sensibility in the Regency image of Rousseau is perhaps most explicitly seen in the career of Robert Southey from the radical rant of *Wat Tyler* to the repressive pieties of a poet laureate. In the preface to his royalist "A Vision of Judgement" (1821) Southey took it upon himself to condemn the satanic "school of poetry," in which Byron was quite obviously demon-in-chief, driven toward the production of his "lascivious books" by a "Satanic spirit of pride and audacious impiety."[25] Making a none-too-subtle appeal to the secular arm, Southey uses the same diabolical imagery on Byron as he does in what one critic has called "some of his most memorable ballads which re-enact the nightmare of being overpowered by an alien will."[26] Damning the satanic school as the work of men possesssed, Southey was himself a man continually fighting against a sensibility that, in retrospect, he confessed to be "a heart full of feeling and poetry, a head full of Rousseau and Werter,"[27] but which, at the time, he indulged on a Jean-Jacques whom he found no less edifying than moving. In 1793 his head was indeed full of the *Confessions*, and he was proud of it:

I have just met with a passage in Rousseau which expresses some of my religious opinions better than I could do it myself. Je ne trouve point de plus doux hommage a la divinite que l'admiration muette qu'excite la contemplation de ses oeuvres. Je ne puis comprendre comment des campagnards et surtout des solitaires peuvent ne pas avoir de foi: comment leur ame ne s'eleve pas cent fois le jour avec extase a l'auteur des merveilles qui les frappent. Dans ma chambre je prie plus rarement et sechement: mais a l'aspect d'un beau paysage je me sens emu. Une vieille femme, pour toute priere, ne savoit dire que O! L'eveque lui dit: Bonne femme, continuez de prier ainsi;

votre priere vaut mieux que les notres,—cette meilleure priere est
aussi la mienne.[28]

What the young Southey saw of himself in passages like this,
hindsight was to view as mindless and characterless emotional-
ism, the deceptively benign symptoms of what he himself
would diagnose as a sensibility of "mimosa."[29] For such a
pathological condition the remedy was the self-control Southey
went on to erect as the ruling value no less of his life than of his
politics, and as a consequence of this reactive formation, not
only did he put behind him his youthful enthusiasm for Rousseau, he also turned his wrath against what Rousseau had
meant to him. For that demonic energy that the pen of Rousseau seemed both to embody and to incite, that egotist excess of
sensibility which linked Rousseau to Byron—that became the
object of Southey's fearful detestation, and we may suspect that
he called it satanic in Byron because, as a vulnerably young
reader of Rousseau and *Werther*, he himself had experienced it
as a demonic overpowering—an annihilation of what ought to
have been, even then, a morally autonomous personality.

Only the young Southey was interested in Rousseau, and the
Rousseau whom he then read and cherished was not the *philosophe*. Indeed, he was something Southey himself defined (very
Rousseauistically) as the diametric opposite of the philosopher.
In a letter inveighing against the "artifice and vanity" of philosophy, he writes that Rousseau "was called a philosopher
whilst he possessed sensibility the most poignant."[30] Likewise
significant is the conclusion to "Romance," an unpublished
poem, written in 1795: an invocation to Rousseau in which the
latter is sensibility's most recent avatar and the young English
poet the next in succession, asking the "guide of his life" to
continue his "divine aid" so that he too may "glow with fire
. . . and strike the soothing lyre."[31] And finally in 1796,
Southey writes his one public tribute to Rousseau, "For the
Cenotaph at Ermenonville":

> Stranger! the MAN of NATURE lies not here:
> Enshrined far distant by his rival's [Voltaire's] side
> His relics rest, there by the giddy throng

With blind idolatry alike revered:
Wiselier directed have thy pilgrim feet
Explored the scenes of Ermenonville. ROUSSEAU
Loved these calm haunts of Solitude and Peace;
Here he has heard the murmurs of the stream,
And the soft rustling of the poplar grove,
When o'er their bending boughs the passing wind
Swept a grey shade. Here, if thy breast be full,
If in thine eye the tear devout should gush,
HIS SPIRIT shall behold thee, to thine home
From hence returning, purified of heart.[32]

As conventional as this sonnet no doubt is, it does seek to make
a distinction that the subsequent conventional widsom about
Rousseau would rarely admit. Here Rousseau is explicitly not
the *philosophe* revered by the revolutionaries who have trans-
ferred his remains to the Pantheon. He is instead the man of
sensibility, associated with nature's "calm haunts of Solitude
and Peace," speaking to full breasts, and inundating them with
tears both devout and purifying.

The purpose of Southey's inscription was to save its subject
from his increasingly assumed association both with Voltaire
and with the "giddy throng" of the Revolution. The strategy
enacting that purpose was to make a distinction both intellectual and moral: look for Rousseau not in Paris but in Ermenonville. Both purpose and strategy, however, were powerless
against the massive weight of an English opinion mobilized
into Rousseauphobia by Burke and repeatedly compressing
Voltaire and Rousseau into one ideological bogeyman. And so,
to an innately febrile sensibility that had always detested Voltaire, the two putative sources of the Revolution became not
alike revered but alike rejected, a process expedited in Southey
by his growing awareness that his sensibility had indeed needed
curbing and that he had achieved a necessary restraint precisely by applying to the trembling pathologies of Rousseau
and *Werther* the rocklike antidotes of Epictetus and Christian
patience.

To Southey young, Rousseau had been all sentiment and
nature. To Southey older, the author of the *Confessions* became

a folly of his youth, put behind him and mocked from the height of a maturity whose distinguishing feature was a self-discipline of iron. In short, that Rousseau whom one might have distinguished from the *philosophes*, that Rousseau whom Southey did once so distinguish, became, even to him, a personal embarrassment if not indeed a public danger. He was not to be spoken of except in that past tense reserved for youthful indiscretions:

I left Westminster in a perilous state,—a heart full of feeling and poetry, a head full of Rousseau and Werter, and my religious principles shaken by Gibbon: many circumstances tended to give me a wrong bias, none to lead me right, except adversity, the wholesomest of all discipline. An instinctive modesty, rather than any purer cause, preserved me for a time from all vice. A severe system of stoical morality then came to its aid. I made Epictetus, for many months, literally my manual.[33]

Much of what a stoical Southey repressed the second generation of English romantics would aggressively resurrect, and one thing they unearthed was Rousseau as man of feeling. For if Southey's manifest fear of Byron was implicitly an effort to clamp down on the personally experienced dangers of a quasi-Rousseauean sensibility, then he had good reason to fear the demonic legions of Byron and his kind, one of whose distinguishing features was their insistent probing toward a more personal and a more complicated Rousseau, his affinities with sentiment and imagination neither dismissed nor reduced but eagerly explored. For Byron and Shelley were always trying to create precursors. They conscripted Milton into the devil's party, and they rediscovered a Rousseau very much like themselves and very different from the standard notion of a *philosphe*.

III

Approaching their artistic maturity at the close of the Napoleonic wars, both Byron and Shelley were politically to the left, socially cosmopolitan, and sensually adventurous. Although they must have been constantly exposed to the facile rigidities

of Burkean denunciation, they were less apt than Wordsworth
to fix themselves into such a manifestly partisan alloy of
personal prudery and theoretical dismissal. Shelley captures
one aspect of the new spirit when, in his *Peter Bell the Third*
(1818), he graphically mocks Wordsworth as a "moral eunuch
/ [who] touched the hem of Nature's shift, / Felt faint—and
never dared uplift / The closest, all-concealing tunic." Its hell
"a city much like London," Shelley's parody of a Wordsworth
double damned for imaginative impotence restricts itself to an
English terrain, but implicit in the Church and Crown dullness
attributed to the "formal puritan / A solemn and unsexual
man," is that self-censorship into which Wordsworth's politics
led him—the Burkean insularity that turned a deaf ear and a
stereotyping anger against the "philosophic gallantry" of the
French Enlightenment.

An Byron and Shelley were poets as much European as English.
After 1815, there became available to them not only a new
world for travel and exile but also a more complex and inward-
ly sympathetic version of recent European history—one in
which it became possible to place the "senti-sensualism" of
Rousseau at the source of the French Revolution but not necessary either to blame it for, or to identify it with Napoleon's lust
for power.

An end for English warriors, Waterloo was a beginning for
English letters. It opened up an entire continent from the not
quite all-concealing tunic that had been stitched together by
propaganda mills professing to be alarmed not only for their
sceptered isle but for morality itself. In 1816, two unconven-
tional Englishmen wrote of Rousseau in a way both more probing and more sympathetic than what had become their compatriots' custom. They were William Hazlitt, writing in Leigh
Hunt's *Examiner*, and Lord Byron, whose Childe Harold now
resumed his pilgrimage by treading "on an Empire's dust" all
the way from Waterloo to Rome—with a long stop at Geneva
where "[Rousseau] became a being."

Byron's portrait of Rousseau in stanzas 76–84 of *Childe
Harold*, 3, is comprehensive in a way that might suggest deriva-

tion from the commonplaces of English prejudice. In just seven stanzas he manages to include: vanity, sophistry, self-pity, emotional masochism, eloquence, verbal wizardry, sensibility, idealism, sensuality, paranoia, insanity, social and political revolution, and selfishness. Scarcely a single count of the usual indictment is left out, and for this conservative reviewers were appreciative. At the *Quarterly* and in his best High Tory manner, Walter Scott praised Byron for the emphasis he had given to vanity as Rousseau's obsessive motivation.[34] At the *Edinburgh*, Jeffrey, while he shared Byron's enchantment with the "Apostle of Love," thought that Byron had done his work "strongly [i.e., negatively] but charitably."[35]

Byron's portrait does indeed direct a good deal of personal criticism at the "self-torturing sophist, wild Rousseau." But the Rousseau of *Childe Harold* is a figure cast in the image of its hero and author—a writer in whom private failings are not only the price of ideal energies but also the medium for public benefits. A mundane vehicle for prophetic powers, Byron's Rousseau is the suffering servant of an energy that destroys himself as well as the ancien régime. Both "kindled" and "blasted" by an "etherial fire," the Rousseau of Byron not only creates the "ideal beauty" of *Julie* but also (and precisely through such visions of excellence) makes the old political order intolerable, toppling kingdoms and making a "wreck of old opinions." Because of him, "mankind has felt their strength and made it felt."

Admitting all of Rousseau's faults, Byron nonetheless names the man himself "all fire" and the man's purest epiphany the passionate but ideal eroticism of *Julie*. Such a characterization reverses the usual emphasis of English opinion. It acknowledges the tainted life of the man only to exalt further the productions of the poet. It also puts the fiery idealism of Rousseau into striking moral contrast with the icy cynicism of Napoleon, whose "great error," according to Byron, "was a continual obtrusion on mankind of his want of all community of feeling for or with them."[36] Byron does not ignore the squabbling misanthrope he found in Grimm's *Correspondance littéraire*—he

whose "mind / Had grown Suspicion's sanctuary"—but he
sees this pathetic figure as an aberration to be distinguished
from the creative "phrensy" that could issue in

> . . . ideal beauty which became
> In him existence, and o'erflowing teems
> Along his burning page, distemper'd though it seems.
>
> (*Childe Harold*, 3. 78. 7–9)

The reason that a revolution so imagined could begin with *La
Nouvelle Héloïse* but end up with the Corsican despot is not hard
to find in *Childe Harold*. In a coda to the stanzas on Rousseau,
Byron versifies the standard liberal explanation that the enslaved French simply were not ready for the ideal beauty offered them by Rousseau:

> . . . pity ceased to melt
> With her once natural charities. But they,
> Who in oppression's darkness caved had dwelt,
> They were not eagles, nourish'd with the day;
> What marvel then, at times, if they mistook their prey.
>
> (3.83.5–9)

But Rousseau having spoken, his energy is still benevolently
latent in the very midst of European reaction:

> In his lair
> Fix'd Passion holds his breath, until the hour
> Which shall atone for years; none need despair:
> It came, it cometh, and will come,—the power
> To punish or forgive—in *one* we shall be slower.
>
> (3.84.5–9)

The fictional Harold is himself one such lair for the cleansing
passion epitomized by Rousseau. So too, perhaps, is the real
Byron. Although he denied it, the apparent similarity between
Byron and Rousseau was an assertion repeatedly made in the
English press. *Blackwood's* called him a "patrician Rousseau."[37]
The *Longon Magazine* called them twin masters of a "minute
moral anatomy" of the self.[38] And in 1816, when the fourth
canto of *Childe Harold* appeared, John Wilson began his review
for the *Edinburgh* with an extended comparison based on the

inability of either writer to distance himself from his literary product. The works of each, Wilson argued, bore the mark of a personal impress and revealed the urgent need for personal expression. Each had peered so deeply into himself that his writings breathed something of "the mysteries of the framing of man."[39] Such repeated comparisons presuppose a whole cluster of characteristics—egotism, sensibility, isolation, misanthropy—that the cultural arbiters of Regency England saw as interrelated symptoms of a personal pathology now spread to England. John Scott of the *London Magazine* offered the careers of Byron and Rousseau as case histories to illustrate his contention that in practice great sensibility meant a great capacity for pain as well as a great susceptibility to misanthropy. It was no accident, he argued, that two virtuosos of sentiment like Byron and Rousseau were the two historical personages to whom the designation of misanthrope had adhered like the mark of Cain.[40]

What *Childe Harold* dramatized as a latent cultural energy ready to spring into cleansing action was, to more conventional English opinion like the *London Magazine*, simply the Beast, unruly in act and fratricidal in consequence. It was the demon of sensibility over which Southey, for example, had felt duty-bound to exert continuous control. But although general English opinion was increasingly intolerant both of Rousseauean sensibility and Byronic satanism, there were some Englishmen who were beginning (once again) not only to praise the sensibility of Rousseau but also openly to identify themselves with its uncompromising egotism. William Hazlitt, for example, recognized a kindred spirit in a writer who, as he said, "relished all more sharply than his fellows."[41] In the *Examiner* of 14 April 1816 Hazlitt argued that Rousseau's sensibility was the most important fact about his personality, so dominant indeed that it inhibited Rousseau's imagination no less than his reason. According to Hazlitt Rousseau's extreme sensibility was "an acute and even morbid feeling of all that [relates] to his own impressions, to the objects and events of his Life."[42] However much time and effort the author of the *Contrat social* may have spent on abstract reasoning, that was not where his great gift lay. Still less was Rousseau an imaginative man. For Hazlitt defines the work of the imagination as the identification of one's self with another—an impossibility for one so absolutely devoted to himself as the Rousseau whom Hazlitt describes. Hazlitt literally loves *La Nouvelle Héloïse*, but its characters and entire plan he considers in no other light than as a projection of the author's temperament.

Rejoicing in the fact of Rousseau's sensibility, Hazlitt rejoices even more in what he takes to have been its social consequence—the French Revolution. He has Rousseau singing a song of himself so intense that it exploded the entire institutional structure of rank and privilege. After Rousseau's revelations, he insists, men could no longer *not* be restive in their various prisons of class and station:

The adept in this school [the Jacobin] does not so much consider the political injury as the personal insult. This is the way to put the case, to set the true revolutionary leaven, the self-love which is at the bottom of every heart, at work, and this was the way in which Rousseau put it. It then becomes a question between man and man, which there is but one way of deciding.[43]

A political radical, Hazlitt celebrates in Rousseau the beginning of a revolutionary impulse. His sacred book, however, is not the *Contrat social* but the *Confessions*. In a brilliant piece of sympathetic criticism, Hazlitt uncovers the prototypical meaning of a seemingly trivial incident that Rousseau, nevertheless, felt compelled to record in the *Confessions*:

It was this which gave such an effect to Rousseau's writings, that he stamped his own character and the image of his self-love on the public mind—*there* it is, and there it will remain in spite of everything. Had he possessed more comprehension of thought or feeling, it would have only diverted him from his object. But it was the excess of his egotism and his utter blindness to every thing else, that found a corresponding sympathy in the conscious feelings of every human breast, and shattered to pieces the pride of rank and circumstance by the pride of internal worth or upstart pretension. . . . [As a young lackey in Turin he came to] that strong conviction of the disparity between the badge on his shoulders and the aspirations of his soul—the determination, in short, that external situation and advantages are but the mask, and that the mind is the man—armed with which, impenetrable, incorrigible, he went forth conquering and to conquer, and overthrew the monarchy of France and the hierarchies of the earth. Till then, birth and wealth and power were all in all, though but the frame-work or crust that envelopes the man; and what there was in the man himself was never asked, or was scorned and forgot. . . . *Rousseau was the first who held the torch (lighted at the never-dying fire in his own bosom) to the hidden chambers of the mind of man—like another Prometheus, breathed into his nostrils the breath of a new and intellectual life, enraging the Gods of the earth, and made him feel what is due to himself and his fellows.*[44] (emphasis added)

Hazlitt claims that Rousseau "'makes us enter into his feelings as if they had been our own, and we seem to remember every incident and circumstance of his life as if it had happened to ourselves.'"[45] So far as Rousseau thus stimulates the sympathetic imagination, he is to be praised, and this Hazlitt does enthusiastically but not without qualification. For the Rousseau whom Hazlitt describes is, like that of *Childe Harold*, an ambiguous cultural hero. His sensibility is "morbid," and he is not thoroughly satisfying even on Hazlitt's own terms. He had "too great a warmth of natural temperament and a tendency to indulge merely the impulses of passions."[46] Even under Hazlitt's most extravagant eulogies there runs a countercurrent of disapproval. We are told that Rousseau's feelings tyrannized him into a condition of disease, the symptoms of which included the narrowing of his mind, jealousy, excessive egotism, contradiction in his thought, and suspicion in his life.[47] According to Hazlitt, Rousseau never steps outside himself. His imagination scarcely exists at all. Nevertheless, precisely because of the concentrated energy of Rousseau's self-portraiture, he coerces from his reader an imaginative response. The personal fascination he was the first to experience works on others with equal intensity but to an opposite effect. It does not plunge them into an even deeper abyss of narcissism. Rather it frees the readers of Rousseau's story from the prison of their respective selves. Hazlitt views Rousseau almost as if he were a scapegoat to a deity of Selfless Imagination—a banished creature whose peremptory obsession with himself assures others that they shall never be totally possessed by the evil spirit of egotism, that grace shall be extended to them, so long as Rousseau is there "overpowering and absorbing the feelings of his readers."[48]

Mme de Staël expressed a typical continental view of Rousseau when she described the imagination as his dominant power.[49] It is, however, with a pointed and explicit rebuttal of de Staël that Hazlitt broaches the topic of Rousseau.[50] Hazlitt agrees that Rousseau possessed great sensibility, but he denies to him even a whit of imagination. Liberated from the closed universe of mere sensibility, imagination does not perpetually play on the one single note of the egotistical sublime. It knows and realizes the other *as other*. Annoyed at Wordsworth's habit of forcing his sensibility into masquerades of imagination, Hazlitt concludes his Rousseau essay by asserting the English poet's basic identity with the author of the *Confessions*. According to Hazlitt, the only thing that distinguishes Wordsworth from Rousseau is his habit of pretending to be interested in a celandine when he is really interested in nothing but himself. Rousseau, by contrast, does not pretend to even the outward show of imagination. He knows his subject to be himself, and he does not apologize for it or attenuate its brashness.

Hazlitt's essay is a good example of Coleridge's "desynonymization" process in language and thought, a process according to which once blurred notions such as obligation and necessity eventually become sharpened into distinct conceptions.[51] Hazlitt's distinction is evidence that a semantic wedge was beginning to be driven between sensibility and imagination, and hereafter, one finds more and more the contention that Rousseau's genius was in some way "illegitimate,"[52] a matter of mere temperament. Hazlitt himself rather bluntly stated, "His genius was the effect of his temperament."[53] A few years later, *Blackwood's* would dub Rousseau one of "the unfortunate children of temperament, who mistake the fretful irritability of their nerves for a yearning of soul."[54] Further on in its fifteen-page article, "On the Genius and Character of Rousseau," it would write, "*we* attribute his acuteness and morbidity of feeling not to a spirit of refined or superior organization, but to mere physical weakness; nay more, to a distempered state of nerves, brought on by debauchery.''[55]

The fastening of Hazlitt's attention on the *Confessions* is one more symptom of an increasing interest in Rousseau as the unique individual who alone could have produced his writings. In a similar fashion and at a more popular level, everyone of Byron's contemporaries was now looking through Rousseau's works for anything that might be considered self-revelatory. In such an atmosphere, the *Confessions* soon became something other than the least-read book of Hazlitt's complaint,[56] and *La Nouvelle Héloïse* ceased to exist as an independent work of art. It became, instead, an exercise in cryptic autobiography, the proper approach to which was through the events and sentiments of Rousseau's life.

Writing about Rousseau's fiction, Hazlitt repeatedly refers to the passions and affections of the novelist, especially to those feelings the young man experienced for Mme de Warens and the old man of the *Rêveries* still continued to nourish. Hence the distinction between Chambéry and Clarens, between fact and fiction, is almost programmatically ignored, the two coming to stand indistinguishably not so much for a place, real or imagined, as for a mood, a land of heart's desire. The peculiarity of Hazlitt's practice as Rousseauphile resides in this: that he is intent upon Rousseau's life but intent upon it only as seen through the rosy ambience of *La Nouvelle Héloïse*. Hazlitt is not embarrassed by Mme de Warens. Instead he rhapsodizes about the mistress of Chambéry almost as if she were a beautiful fiction, another Julie:

To cherish the writer and *damn* the author is as if the traveller who slakes his thirst at the running stream, should revile the spring-head from which it gushes. I do not speak of the degree of passion felt by Rousseau towards Madame Warens, nor of his treatment of her, nor her's of him: but that he thought of her for years with the tenderest yearnings of affection and regret, and felt towards her all that he has made his readers feel, this I cannot for a moment doubt.[57]

But Hazlitt's identification of Rousseau with St. Preux usually worked to the opposite effect. Rousseau's tawdry relations with

Maman were avidly read but almost universally as a debunking
gloss on the beautiful soul of St. Preux, a comforting revelation
that *La Nouvelle Héloïse* was nothing but a disguise pasted over
the ugly desires of Rousseau's life—just as Burke had said it
was. It was, in fact, to just such an anti-Rousseau tirade that
Hazlitt addressed his warmest defense of Rousseau—"On the
Jealousy and the Spleen of Party."[58] Thomas Moore, who previously had amused himself with the touristy Rousseaumania
of one of the younger Fudges,[59] had, in *Rhymes on the Road*,
called Mme de Warens and Rousseau "strange, low people,
low and bad."[60] Skeletons in the closet of a would-be moralist
were questionable enough, but when Rousseau applied his cosmetic talents to his own shambles of a life, then genius itself
seemed a sinister power:

> Strange power of Genius, that can throw
> Round all that's vicious, weak, and low,
> Such magic lights, such rainbow dyes
> As dazzle even the steadiest eyes.[61]

Moore went on in this way for forty lines, ranting against
Rousseau as a mad pauper and against Mme de Warens as a
veritable "Madam" dividing herself between Jean-Jacques
and her footman. For whatever reason, Moore edited these
lines (5–45) out of the 1841 edition of his poems. By that time
perhaps, the intemperateness of his censure had become something of an embarrassment to him. In any case, he had indeed
written it two decades before, and apparently it did not then
seem overstated to anyone besides Hazlitt. On the contrary, it
was then the typical and expected sequel to any inspection of
Rousseau's life. The eccentric point of view belonged to Hazlitt, the unruly and would-be Promethean voice that kept
insisting on Rousseau's excellence both as man and writer.

Seeking a plausible explanation for the tremendous power of
Rousseau's pen, Hazlitt found one in what, along with Byron,
he conceived to be the impulse of personal passion illuminating
every one of Rousseau's statements, even the ostensibly
abstract. But however appreciative of Rousseau it might have
been, the effect of such an explanation was to reduce to a mere

expression of personal makeup the great and varied achievement of the writer. An avowed disciple of Rousseau, Hazlitt chose for exclusive emphasis precisely that aspect of his master's career that had done the most damage to his reputation. Admiring Rousseau in this manner, he fostered the already strong movement toward a narrowly personal assessment of Rousseau, a movement in which there were very few members other than hostile.

The bad press Rousseau encountered every time attention was drawn to his life may be illustrated by the favorable 1819 reviews of Mme d'Épinay's *Mémoires et correspondance*. This was a work Mme d'Épinay had intended as a *roman à clef* and Grimm (most likely) had edited into a picture of Rousseau even blacker than the one first painted by his estranged patroness. The manuscript did not come to public light until 1818 when Brunet, its editor, restoring as many of the real names as possible, chose to present it as a factual memoir rather than a work of fiction.[62] The vanity and sexual license of the society described by Mme d'Épinay greatly offended her English reviewers. Rousseau, portrayed by Mme d'Épinay as just another inhabitant of this unsavory world, differed from his fellow libertines only in his professions of austerity. In him the vices of the flesh and the world emitted the more pungent odor of hypocrisy. He was a critic of delights the lure of which he could not resist and would not acknowledge. Such equivocal behavior violated even the exiguous code of Mme d'Épinay, who finally condemned Rousseau as a man totally reprehensible because totally false.

English men of letters accepted such condemnation of Rousseau with a remarkable degree of trust, coming as it did from the hands of Rousseau's most implacable enemies. Diderot or Grimm could hardly have put the matter more harshly than did Jeffrey, writing in the pages of one of Britain's most influential and supposedly most liberal journals:

Jean-Jacques Rousseau seems, as the reward of genius and fine writing, to have claimed an exemption from all moral duties. He borrowed, and begged, and never paid;—put his children in a poorhouse—betrayed his friends—insulted his benefactors—and was guilty of every species of meanness and mischief.[63]

Such a grotesque personal image provoked within every student of Rousseau a confrontation between itself and the admirable sentiments of works like *Julie*, *Émile*, and the two discourses. This kind of confrontation accounts for the variously ambivalent judgments Rousseau could provoke in men like Byron and Hazlitt. For in Rousseau, theory and practice seemed to go each their separate ways, daring the observant mind to fit into one coherent shape the two contradictory descriptions of Rousseau the man and Rousseau the writer. Many followed Mme d'Épinay and denounced Rousseau as a hypocrite. Jeffrey was one of these:

[Rousseau] with . . . warmth of imagination, and great professions of philanthropy in his writings, uniformly indicated in his individual character the most irritable, suspicious, and selfish dispositions; and plainly showed, that his affection for mankind was entirely theoretical, and had no living objects in this world.[64]

The New Monthly Review also thought it had found the key to Rousseau: "utter want of coincidence between his theoretical maxims and his temperament and habits."[65] As a young man his character had been irretrievably corrupted. Later on, when he had thought his way through to an intellectual abhorrence of vice, his championship of virtue was, while not quite an attitude, certainly a desperate and impotent effort of the will:

by the time that Rousseau's philosophical opinions were formed, his personal morals were gone; and it was his fate to commence his public career, inveterately attached, by taste and temperament, to many of the licentious indulgences against which he vehemently, and we do think, very sincerely enveighed.[66]

One portrait, appearing in *Blackwood's* (1819) and written by Hazlitt's friend, P. G. Patmore,[67] gives more weight to the writings than to the man. Rather than being a bad man despite his beautiful productions, Rousseau is to *Blackwood's* a good man despite his many lapses. Chambéry and Mme de Warens had been exquisitely adapted to feed the peculiar propensities of his romantic nature.[68] Ultimately, they were productive of the glories of Clarens and *Julie*, the latter proof positive that

they remained with him as the center of his spiritual existence
"no matter where his weak and diseased body might be de-
tained by his still more weak and diseased will."[69] But the
"pollutions of great cities" had damaged Rousseau's imagination, and before his environment he had shown himself to be
too sensitive, too weak:

The moment he sets his foot within the walls of a city, I am obliged to
quit him; for then his spirits sink, his heart shrinks inward to an
obscure corner of his breast, his earthly blood begins to ferment,—
and poor, pitiful bodily self stands forth, and with its soiled and misty
mantle, covers and conceals all things . . . and thus blind and helpless
and miserable, he either lies at the mercy of those who have no
mercy, or, in despair, plunges into the throng and becomes as mean
and as wicked as the rest. . . . Rousseau—the poor, frail, feeble,
Rousseau. . . . There he lay—fettered and imprisoned—groaning
beneath his bondage, without patience to bear or strength to break it
—and every struggle fastening the chains still more closely about him
—till at length the iron entered into his heart and brain, and corrod-
ing there, drove him to distraction:—for such was undoubtedly his
condition at the last.[70]

The Rousseau of wartime England was not an individual.
Deemed to be of the philosophic party, he was simply one of its
members, a quasi-obligatory target for national hostility. His
only distinction was the thoroughness with which he seemed to
illustrate the selfishness and sensuality of foreign ideas. The
Rousseau of post-Napoleonic Europe was, by contrast, an
eruptive force uniquely personal. He was in the words of
Hazlitt, the bearer of that fire that was the unremitting sense of
one's own "internal worth." While such characterizations—
almost always executed in an imagery of fire—did indeed con-
tribute to the increasingly sharp distinction made between
Rousseau and the other *philosophes*, they did not free Jean-
Jacques from English distaste. On the contrary, they drew
detailed and usually horrified attention to a man whose abun-
dantly recorded life had been as weak and irresponsible as his
pen had been energetic and admirable. This was the great
riddle of Rousseau. For while some continued to praise an

essential Rousseau to be found in his books, far more refused to stay within the pure spaces of artistic creation. Instead, they denied the beneficent power of Rousseau's pen and stressed a personal weakness for which Promethean fires on the page were a specious compensation, too uncontrolled to be good and too literary to be true. This was the challenge Shelley eventually confronted in the "Triumph of Life": the easy criticism that a biographically wretched Rousseau seemed not only to invite and verify but also to extend to the imagination itself—a faculty that, as dubiously present in Rousseau, seemed like nothing more than unbridled egotism when "his earthly blood begins to ferment,—and poor, pitiful self stands forth, and with its soiled and misty mantle, covers and conceals all things."

What gave point and urgency to attacks so indistinguishably personal and aesthetic was the still universal assumption that responsibility for the French Revolution was to be laid at the door of a Rousseau either philosophic or sentimental. To be reductionist or cynical about the effect of Rousseau's books— Byron's "tears shed feelingly and fast"—was to side with the furies whom Shelley had torture his Prometheus. It was to insist that the proposed new order was *not* "a legioned band of linked brothers / Whom Love calls children." It was to gloat that the revolutions in polity and sensibility were not the offspring of love but (in the stinging retort of the furies) "another's"—a legion of selfishness which initially could wear the mask of sentiment but had ultimately to reveal its true nature. In 1822 the perceived contradicitons of Rousseau were the contradictions of the French Revolution, and in making Rousseau the protagonist of his "Triumph of Life," Shelley was following the precedent of Byron in *Childe Harold*. He was performing a biopsy on a writer whom the English routinely identified as the prototype of their age both by his reach toward perhaps unattainable heights and by his documented plunge into very real and ignoble depths.

But before arriving at Shelley's final major poem, we must first examine how the developments of his own protracted discovery of Rousseau monadically reflect those of his time and place, mirror these larger developments almost as if meant to illustrate what Shelley himself wrote in his preface to *Prometheus Unbound*:

Every man's mind is . . . modified by all the objects of nature and art; by every word and suggestion which he ever admitted to act upon his consciousness; it is the mirror upon which all forms are reflected, and in which they compose one form. Poets, not otherwise than philosophers, painters, sculptors, and musicians, are, in one sense, the creators, and, in another, the creations, of their age. From this subjection the loftiest do not escape.[71]

About Rousseau, Shelley was brought up in a certain *langue*. He was subjected to a certain grammar the evolving syntax of which we have tried to make plain. It is now our task to see how, necessarily staying within the conventions of that *langue*, Shelley nonetheless moved toward the very original *parole* that is the "Triumph of Life."

4

The Greatest Man since Milton:
Shelley and Rousseau

IN THE spring and summer of 1816, English romantic discussion of Rousseau becomes suddenly abundant. William Hazlitt's "On the Character of Rousseau" appears in the *Examiner* for 14 April and within three months, Byron likewise holds forth on the subject in the third canto of *Childe Harold*, a poem composed in the suggestive ambience of Lake Geneva. And coming out of the same stimulating milieu is Shelley's contribution—a long epistolary account of his and Byron's voyage around the perimeter of the lake.

The three compositions may be related. Each successive effort may have been written with an awareness of what preceded. Byron and Shelley were both readers of the *Examiner*, and they were both still in England for the issue containing Hazlitt's essay. In Switzerland, the two poets were constant companions, and when finally they did part, Shelley returned to England, personally delivering the manuscript of *Childe Harold* to Byron's publisher. But as suggestive and plausible as such links may be, the fact remains that going to Shelley from Byron and Hazlitt is like traveling back more than a half-century to the first enthusiastic reception of *La Nouvelle Héloïse*. For that work and the "divine imagination" animating it are Shelley's exclusive concern.

Shelley's letter is so empty of personal scandal that it suggests ignorance of it—a suggestion not unsupported by Mary's rather extensive record of her husband's reading, in which there is only one entry for an autobiographical work by Rousseau. In 1815 Shelley read the *Rêveries*.[1]

When he was only eighteen, however, Shelley did write a letter containing a direct reference to the *Confessions*. In reply to a literary proposal of T. J. Hogg's that they jointly write something autobiographical, Shelley responded, "The *Confessions* of Rousseau are the only thing of the kind that have appeared, & they are either a disgrace to the confessor or a string of falsehoods, probably the latter."[2] The motive imputed for the second, favored alternative is the orthodox wisdom about Rousseau—a vanity so strong that he would gladly accuse himself of any sort of imaginary baseness so long as it drew attention to himself. While the reference confirms that Shelley knew, at least vaguely, the facts of the *cas Rousseau*, it does not constitute any evidence that Shelley had, at this point, actually read the *Confessions*. On the contrary, the nature of Shelley's brief allusion, its banal repetition of reactionary condemnation, strikes one as grossly incongruous coming from the pen of the young "atheist" just expelled from Oxford. Radical as he most assuredly was, even Shelley was not immune to the received ideas on Rousseau, ideas that masked their reactionary and anti-Revolutionary intent behind the cloak of personal moral censure.

It is probable that Shelley excluded personal history from his letter at Lake Geneva not because he was totally ignorant of that history but because it did not interest him, absorbed as he was by the sublimities of *La Nouvelle Héloïse*. Such a direction in Shelley's attention would be consistent with his habitual attitude toward those creative minds whom he included under the broadly inclusive title of poets. "Let us assume," he asserts, "that Homer was a drunkard, that Vergil was a flatterer, that Horace was a coward, that Tasso was a madman, that Lord Bacon was a peculator, that Raphael was a libertine, that Spenser was a poet laureate. . . . Their errors have been weighed and found to have been dust in the balance."[3] Supremely indifferent to worldly dross, Shelley collects and

treasures only the purest alloy of vision. No clouds of personality—neither questionable motives nor unfortunate consequences—darken his radiant celebration of a Julie who is not
only the ideal of Rousseau's imagination but also the ideal of
the French Revolution.

Introducing his subject in 1816, Shelley is unintentionally
ambiguous about his previous familiarity with *La Nouvelle
Héloïse*. He writes, "It is nearly a fortnight since I have returned from Vevai. This journey has been on every account
delightful, but more especially, because then I first knew the
divine beauty of Rousseau's imagination, as it exhibits itself in
Julie."[4] Had he never before read the book? Or was he express-
ing nothing more than what he definitely does say in the letter:
that a new splendor flashes from the novel when read in the
beauty of its natural setting? Mary's unequivocal statement
that this was indeed the first reading is not wholly reliable,
written as it was almost a quarter-century later, and being perhaps merely her interpretation of what Shelley has written in
the letter.[5] While justification for a contrary opinion is not per-
suasive, it is not altogether lacking. For in a letter as early as
1811, Shelley does mention the characters of the novel, but the
nineteen-year old's egregiously mistaken identification of St.
Preux would seem to indicate that Shelley had then only heard
of *La Nouvelle Héloïse*, not read it.[6]

One cannot be certain about Shelley's pre-1816 acquaintance with *La Nouvelle Héloïse*. But whether Shelley had or had
not previously read *Julie* is essentially irrelevant and unimpor-
tant. The important fact and novelty is a fact and novelty of
Shelley's consciousness: before 1816 his awareness of *La
Nouvelle Héloïse* is minimal; after that date the novel occupies a
privileged place in his mind. Shelley's reading *in situ* of *La
Nouvelle Héloïse* marks a dramatic turning point in the course of
his notions about Rousseau. Before his pilgrimage to the land
of Julie and St. Preux there are indeed several references to
Rousseau, both in Shelley's published works and in his private
correspondence. They do not allude, however, to the creator of
La Nouvelle Héloïse. Nor do they have much to say about the
notorious celebrity or about the innovative historian of himself.

Rather, Shelley directs his attention almost exclusively to
Rousseau's membership in that band of mostly French writers
whose critical philosophy was constantly being discovered at
the origin of the French Revolution.

To the younger Shelley, Rousseau was merely another *philosophe*. He was no more than a junior partner in an enterprise
whose greater lights the notes to *Queen Mab* identify as mechan-
ists such as Holbach, Helvétius, and Godwin. The eighteen-
year old Shelley's first recorded judgment on Rousseau goes so
far as to compose a list of "deist" iconclasts in which Rousseau
is classed with such kindred spirits as Voltaire and David
Hume.[7] Such blithe ignorance of the fundamental quarrels
separating Jean-Jacques from his Enlightenment peers argues
persuasively for Shelley's initially rather incomplete awareness
either of Rousseau's uniqueness or of his complexity. Furthermore, the following boastful remark could not possibly have
issued from the mouth of anyone even slightly familiar with the
numerous dents in Rousseau's reputation: "the life of all of
them was characterized by the strictest morality; all of them
whilst they lived were the subjects of panegyric, were the direc-
tors of literature & morality."[8] The most notorious of egotists,
Rousseau was, to the young Shelley, scarcely an individual at
all. He was little more than a member of a class. Within a
decade, however, Shelley was to arrive at an idea of Rousseau,
insistent in its particularity. For by that time Shelley would be
categorically describing Rousseau as "essentially a poet,"
claimed for his "Defence of Poetry" and reclaimed from the
French Enlightenment. Shelley began this process of reclamation in 1816, when he read *La Nouvelle Héloïse*.

II

About Jean-Jacques's spotless moral credentials young
Shelley was soon disabused. His letter to Hogg, written only a
few months after his inclusion of Rousseau among the "direc-
tors of . . . morality," describes the author of the *Confessions*, in
pure commonplace, as either a disgrace or a monstrous liar. A
year later the political missionary to Ireland does not stop at

honoring Rousseau as one among many forerunners of the French Revolution. In addition, he finds an unflattering place for him in his apology for revolutionary failure. Along with similar strictures on Voltaire, Helvétius, and Condorcet, he writes the following about Rousseau:

[He] gave license by his writings to passions that only incapacitate and contract the human heart. So far hath he prepared the necks of his fellow-beings for that yoke of galling and dishonourable servitude which at this moment it bears.[9]

This is Shelleyan for the cliché about Rousseau's egotism and sensuality, Shelley's use of it most probably deriving from the respectably radical and enlightened judgments Mary Woll-stonecraft had delivered against Rousseau in *A Vindication of the Rights of Women.* As this example illustrates, the personal obloquy attached to Rousseau's name could be useful even in the polemics of an English Jacobin. If Edmund Burke could damn the Revolution by associating it with Rousseau, Shelley was likewise capable of using that same association to explain away the political disappointment defining the post-Revolutionary era in which he wrote. Shelley's argument was that the *philosophes* were essentially right but not totally right. This being the case, it should not have been cause for either surprise or despair that the Revolution itself turned out to be a house-cleaning that in its concrete development was something less than totally admirable.

With *Queen Mab* (1813) one comes to positive and definite evidence not only that Shelley knew Rousseau's work but that he approached it with the special and restricted interest of a radical social scientist. The notes to the poem contain two foot-note references to Rousseau. For the assertion that employ-ments are lucrative in an inverse ratio to their usefulness, Shelley directs the reader to "Rousseau, De l'Inégalité parmi les Hommes, note 7."[10] Discussing the high infant mortality rate, supposedly caused by the toxic milk of mothers fed on "dead flesh," Shelley notes, "See also *Emile,* chap. i, pp. 53,54,56."[11] Furthermore, in an appendix to the *Vindication of*

Natural Diet, later deleted from the *Queen Mab* note, the 113 years of vegetation Patrick O'Neale are footnoted, "*Emile*, I.44."[12] The reference to "note 7" of the inequality discourse is clearly an error. It is Rousseau's ninth note to which reference should have been made. The verbal similarity, amounting to translation, is conclusive. For Shelley's "No greater evidence is afforded of the wide extended and radical mistakes of civilized man than this fact: those arts which are essential to his very being are held in the greatest contempt; employments are lucrative in an inverse ratio to their usefulness"[13] we have Rousseau's "en général les Arts sont lucratifs en raison inverse de leur utilité, et . . . les plus nécessaires doivent enfin devenir les plus négligés."[14] The two references to *Émile* are more puzzling. It is uncertain what edition of *Émile* Shelley may have been using. It ought to be one (undiscovered by this writer) in which the Patrick O'Neale reference occurs on page 44, and in which pages 53, 54, 56 relate to the effects of diet on a mother's milk. Further complicating an investigation of Shelley's borrowings from Rousseau is the theory of the former's unacknowledged indebtedness to Joseph Ritson's *An Essay on Abstinence from Animal Food as a Moral Duty* (1802) convincingly argued by David Lee Clark.[15] It would seem that the entire appendix to the *Vindication of Natural Diet* (and with it, the footnote reference to *Emile* 1.44) was lifted from Ritson, pp. 148–152. Although this points towards the possibility of Shelley's ignorance of *Emile* 1, it still does not account for the other references to *Emile* 1.53,54,56. In any event, by November, 1813, Shelley had most certainly read *Le Discours sur l'inégalité* and most probably the first book of *Émile*, if not the entire work.

Shelley's early borrowings from Rousseau are practical and specific in nature. For him Rousseau is a competent specialist who can present a technical economic argument against civilized luxury or propound the nutritional requirements for nursing mothers. The Rousseau of the young Shelley is one of many precise French thinkers, not the uniquely powerful creator of the sentimental classic, *La Nouvelle Héloïse*. Indeed, to the young Shelley, Rousseau is never an individual. He is, rather, only one of several deists, only one of several forerunners of the revolution, only one of several authorities for the manifestoes of *Queen Mab*. He is always a particle of enlightened humanity, never that peculiar article called Jean-Jacques Rousseau.

Within his narrow field of interest, however, Shelley struck to the very heart of Rousseau's social criticism:

No greater evidence is afforded of the wide extended and radical mistakes of civilized man than this fact: those arts which are essential to his very being are held in the greatest contempt; employments are lucrative in an inverse ratio to their usefulness: [Shelley's note: "See Rousseau, *De l'inégalité parmi les Hommes*, note 7."] the jeweller, the toyman, the actor gains fame and wealth by the exercise of his useless and ridiculous art; whilst the cultivator of the earth, he without whom society must cease to subsist, struggles through contempt and penury, and perishes by that famine which but for his unceasing exertions would annihilate the rest of mankind.[16]

What Shelley learned from Rousseau was the effective critical technique of cultural primitivism. Like Rousseau, he imagined the strengths and beauties of less sophisticated ways of life; like Rousseau, he did so in an effort to cast doubt on the rectitude of civilized things as they were.

Shelley's indebtedness to Rousseau can be most clearly seen in two early novels of his friend, Thomas Love Peacock, each of which contains a major character modeled on Shelley as the latter must have appeared in his salad days in the Newton and Boinville circles. Escot and Sylvan Forester, the *raisonneurs* respectively of *Headlong Hall* and *Melincourt*, are both cultural primitivists, mounted astride a radical hobbyhorse whose pedigree the novelist reveals to us in numerous footnote references to Rousseau's two discourses. Satire very often alchemizes even the well-intentioned radical into a crank, but this is not what Peacock does with his Shelley surrogates. Escot and Forester each occupy the ethical center of their respective fictions. It is true that Sylvan Forester's noble anthropoid, Sir Oran Haut-ton, mocks the pages of Monboddo and Rousseau, but it is equally true that Peacock's playful presentation of the ape as a gracious knight-errant, sensitive to the beauties of music and superior in heart to the English gentry, catches in brilliant wit the point about overrefinement which Rousseau's earnestness often confused into an unintended and absurd invitation to fall down on all fours and chew the nearest acorn.

The criticizing bent of Peacock's Shelleyan characters accords perfectly with Shelley's own judgments about the "mistakes of civilized man," and that Shelley used the technique of cultural primitivism with a full awareness of its potential for absurdity should be sufficiently clear from what he wrote about Rousseau in his "Essay on Christianity":

Nothing is more obviously false than that the remedy of inequality among men consists in their return to the condition of savages and beasts. Philosophy will never be understood if we approach the study of its mysteries with so narrow and illiberal conceptions of its universality. Rousseau certainly did not mean to persuade the immense population of his country to abandon all the arts of life, destroy their habitations and their temples and become the inhabitants of the woods. He addressed the most enlightened of his compatriots, and endeavored to persuade them to set the example of a pure and simple life, by placing in the strongest point of view his conceptions of the calamitous and diseased aspect which, overgrown as it is with the vices of sensuality and selfishness, is exhibited by civilized society.[17]

To the young Shelley Rousseau was a social reformer who, with "more connected and systematic enthusiasm [than Christ]," raged against the luxury of men and for the equality of mankind.[18] Apparently, at this writing, Rousseau the poet had not yet been made manifest to Shelley.

There is some probability that as early as 1815 Shelley began to extend his narrow conception of Rousseau. As already noted, one of Mary's reading lists records that sometime during that year Shelley did indeed read one non-*philosophe* work of Rousseau's—*Les Rêveries du promeneur solitaire*. And just the previous summer Shelley had set Claire Clairmont "a task to translate from one of Rousseau's *Rêveries*," an assignment which suggests that his interest in the *Rêveries* was something more than casual.[19] Indeed, thematic similarities between this

work and Shelley's *Alastor* (1815) have led at least two French
scholars and, more recently, an American to speculate on the
possibility that in *Alastor* Shelley was attentive to Rousseau as,
mutatis mutandis, a visionary poet.[20]

A treasury of ecstatic experience, the *Rêveries* are also an
unguarded expression of one of Rousseau's most notorious
foibles—his willful pursuit of misanthropic and paranoid solitude. Solipsistic in the extreme, the *Rêveries* act upon their
author like imaginative irritants: they goad him into his completed state as both seer and misanthrope. They are, therefore,
an intensified personalization of precisely the ambivalence that
one finds in the fictional protagonist of *Alastor*. The subtitle of
Alastor is *The Spirit of Solitude*, and its preface describes its
visionary hero as a "self-centered" egotist, justly and fatally
avenged by the "spirit of sweet human love." At the conclusion of the poem, however, its protagonist is eulogized as a sur-
passing spirit whose death has left the world poorer. The poet
of *Alastor* is, therefore, brother to Rousseau as solitary walker:
he is both derelict and visionary.

Shelley's ambivalent attitude toward his own character may
or may not reflect a similar ambivalence toward the subject-
author of the *Rêveries*, but any identification of Rousseau as the
poet of *Alastor* would be merely another fruitless overspecifica-
tion of Shelley's theme. Shelley himself describes *Alastor* as
"allegorical of one of the most interesting situations of the
human mind." Certain individuals—Wordsworth, Coleridge,
Shelley himself—may be instances of the *Alastor* type, but
instances and personalities are not the focus of Shelley's attention. He is not a doctor diagnosing a patient but a biologist
seeking to define a generic morphology.

One should not, however, slight the striking congruities that
do exist between *Alastor* and the *Rêveries*. It is not only that both
works provoke the same kind of ambivalent response but also
that the polarities of the ambivalence are in both cases the
powers of vision and the catastrophes of egotism. Rousseau as
he appears in the *Rêveries* undoubtedly represents one instance
of this visionary-egotist type, but all the evidence suggests that
it is an instance not yet fully present to Shelley when he writes

Alastor. For such a conscious intention on Shelley's part would indicate that, already in 1815, Rousseau was for Shelley a visionary *manqué*, a poet done in by his own egotism. Such indeed was to be the problematic role assigned Rousseau in "The Triumph of Life," but Shelley's last work, is, I would contend, a deliberate refashioning of the *Alastor* theme, a refashioning necessitated by precisely what nothing in the record shows to have been true of Shelley when he wrote *Alastor* —an awareness of Jean-Jacques Rousseau as a quite different paradigm for the defeats of an imaginative man.

Up until 1816, Shelley did not consider Rousseau as anything like a visionary poet. His pre-1816 notion is that Rousseau is a *philosophe*, and when he does finally discover *La Nouvelle Héloïse*, his response is to fix his attention on "the divine beauty of Rousseau's imagination,"[21] give voice to a full-throated hymn of praise, and generally act as if everything either philosophic or embarrassing about Rousseau has been declared inadmissible. So great and sudden is this change in Shelley's idea of Rousseau that one may legitimately speak of it as a conversion. No longer the logic-chopping *philosophe*, Shelley's Rousseau will now become an inspired hierophant. He will become a poet, a poet who, for the moment at least, was untouched by the ambivalence and sorrow of *Alastor*.

III

Fully the final third of Shelley's 1816 letter to Peacock is taken up with the last two stops of his trip—Clarens, the scene of *La Nouvelle Héloïse*, and Ouchy near Lausanne where Edward Gibbon composed his monumental history of Roman decadence. As Shelley recounts his two-day stay at Clarens, his actions no less than his words become quite effusive. On his first trip to the *bosquet de Julie* he pleads guilty to a grave sin of omission:

Why did the cold maxims of the world compel me at this moment to repress the tears of melancholy transport which it would have been so sweet to indulge, immeasurably, even until the darkness of night had swallowed up the objects which excited them?[22]

But amendment is quick: the very next day he gathers some roses which "might be the posterity of some planted by Julie's hand."[23]

Byron and Shelley subsequently move on to Lausanne and the summerhouse where Gibbon completed *The Decline and Fall of the Roman Empire*. But this time it is only Byron who stops to gather memorial flowers, the species in this instance being the acacia under the cover of which Gibbon had privately celebrated the completion of his life's work. Shelley deliberately withholds a similar tribute, and he insists on telling us why. He will not gather flowers in Gibbon's name, he tells us, because the latter is unworthy to share the same pedestal as Rousseau:

My companion gathered some acacia leaves to preserve in remembrance of him. I refrained from doing so, fearing to outrage the greater and more sacred name of Rousseau; the contemplation of whose imperishable creations had left no vacancy in my heart for mortal things. Gibbon had a cold and unimpassioned spirit. I never felt more inclination to rail at the prejudices which cling to such a thing, than now that Julie and Clarens, Lausanne and the Roman Empire, compelled me to a contrast between Rousseau and Gibbon.[24]

The refusal to do equal floral honors to Gibbon is, to be sure, a theatrical gesture. Be that as it may and however unsuccessful Shelley's gesture may be, it is at least clear what he meant by it. He meant to reinforce the letter's most fundamental assertion about the imagination and its priority to "reality." Sharpening the cutting edge of the explicitly stated distinction between Rousseau and Gibbon, Shelley's act dramatizes a notion as old as Aristotle—that poetry is the epistemological superior of history.

The letter comes to a close immediately after the explicit comparison of Rousseau and Gibbon, and it is an ending that sounds in the ear like a resolving chord:

When we returned, in the only interval of sunshine during the day, I walked on the pier which the lake was lashing with its waves. A rainbow spanned the lake, or rather rested one extremity of its arch upon the water, and the other at the foot of the mountains of Savoy. Some white houses, I know not if they were those of Meillerie, shone through the yellow fire.[25]

Less reportage than emblem, this paragraph is the earliest instance (and perhaps the origin) of a recurring Shelleyan symbol, the best-known variant of which imagines life as a many colored dome of glass staining the white radiance of eternity. Insofar as Shelley's poetry is visionary, it is a constant effort to shatter that many colored dome of glass; and it is the (perhaps) white-hot energy of his imagination which is supposed to do the job. By contrast, piecing together chromatic splinters is, for Shelley, the ambition of a menial who, having stolen the title of reason, is rather too given to puffing himself up with a string of certain but petty triumphs.

Now, if anyone may be said to have been a man of the Enlightenment, it was the author of *The Decline and Fall of the Roman Empire*, and it is clear that Shelley's 1816 letter to Peacock is, to a great extent, merely a loaded comparison between Rousseau and the "cold and unimpassioned spirit" of Gibbon. The reason for what Shelley himself calls such "railing" was the subjective novelty of the contrast. It was the first time he had distinguished Rousseau from his Enlightenment peers. And once Shelley did discover Rousseau as a poetic novelist, he could never again consider him just another rationalist. Instead, he would usually go out of his way to emphasize the uniqueness of Jean-Jacques. When Peacock argued that the reasoner was superior to the poet, Shelley not only opposed the general principle but also denied that Rousseau was an appropriate illustration of Peacock's case, and he could not forbear the following footnote on the association of Locke, Hume, Gibbon, Voltaire, and Rousseau—Peacock's list of intellectual heroes: "I follow the classification adopted by the author of *The Four Ages of Poetry*. Although Rousseau has been thus classed, he was essentially a poet. The others, even Voltaire, were mere reasoners."[26]

After his 1816 reading of *La Nouvelle Héloïse*, Shelley never failed to exempt Rousseau from his habitual and inclusive disparagement of French literature as "weak, superficial, vain, with little imagination, and with passions as well as judgments cleaving to the external form of things.''[27] Whether justly or not, Shelley came to identify French letters with only the most superficial kind of rationalism. When, only a year before his death, he outlined a course of literary study, he concluded with the following gratuitous observation: ''The French language you, like every other respectable woman, already know; and if the great name of Rousseau did not redeem it, it would have been perhaps as well that you remained entirely ignorant of it.''[28] Such pointed statements about Rousseau's uniqueness— his distinctiveness from other French writers as well as from all ''mere reasoners''—are the natural language of the convert atoning for his previous blindness and lack of discrimination. After 1816, ''Rousseau is indeed in my mind the greatest man the world has produced since Milton.''[29]

Having discovered that Rousseau was quite different from the usual denizens of a Parisian *salon*, Shelley did not there-upon ignore either Rousseau's intellectual significance or his didactic essays.[30] To Shelley, indeed, Rousseau the poet was an even more revolutionary figure than Rousseau the ideo-logue. Upon his death, Shelley writes, ''the French nation should have enjoined a public mourning.''[31] But it is sensibility that is now seminal, not political and social theory. From Maria Louisa's journey to the scenes of *La Nouvelle Héloïse*, Shelley infers a shift in sensibility, which is prior to and genera-tive of social and political reality:

How beautiful it is to find that the common sentiments of human nature can attach themselves to those who are the most removed from its duties and its enjoyments, when Genius pleads for their admission at the gate of Power. . . . A Bourbon dared not even to have remem-bered Rousseau. She owed this power to that democracy which her husband's [i.e., Napoleon's] dynasty outraged, and of which it was however, in some sort, the representative among the nations of the earth. This little incident shows at once how unfit and how impossible it is for the ancient system of opinions, or for any power built upon a conspiracy to revive them, permanently to subsist among mankind.[32]

When the ''Defence'' defines the nature of Rousseau's

achievement (as belatedly appreciated by Shelley), that definition has scarcely anything to do with critical acumen. Rather, Rousseau is one of those poets who "have celebrated the dominion of love, planting as it were trophies in the human mind of that sublimest victory over sensuality and force."[33] This, Shelley came to believe, is the only true revolution, the only real triumph.

In closing his letter to Peacock, Shelley does not stop at a description of the rainbow. He also points toward a radiance that shines through it—the white houses on the opposite shore. That Shelley knows not whether these houses are situated at Meillerie is an agnosticism urbanely appropriate to Intellectual Beauty, who grants only shadowy and inconstant visits. Geographically, Meillerie is the promontory on Lake Geneva where St. Preux wrote one of the most famous and most passionate letters in *La Nouvelle Héloïse*. Banished from Julie's sight and toying with suicide, he *imagines* his beloved on the farther shore. Shelley pithily describes the situation as one of "visionary exile."[34] Palaces of vision, the houses shining through Shelley's rainbow are radiantly white, their whiteness and the rainbow through which they shine being a figure not only for the relation of Rousseau to Gibbon, but also of Rousseau to the entire Enlightenment, and of poetry to history.

Shelley's letter repeatedly demotes "reality" in favor of the imagination. The antithesis of icy Gibbon is a Rousseauean warmth, "a mind so powerfully bright as to cast a shade of falsehood on the records that are called reality," the records the historian of the Roman Empire so devotedly served. As Rousseau and the fiction of Julie d'Etange go together, so too do Gibbon and the facts of Imperial Rome which Shelley more than once deplored as a spiritual and cultural disaster. The large design according to which Shelley defines his polarities forces Gibbon into a strange alliance with the monks who have destroyed the *bosquet de Julie*. The anti-Rousseauism of the monks is as act brutally obtuse and as symbol crudely obvious. Gibbon, by contrast, distinguishes himself from Rousseau less by the bludgeon applied to the sacred bower than by the rapier of his justly celebrated irony. But these are, to Shelley, but

different varieties of coldness. The style is different; the anti-
Rousseau temperature remains the same. A chronicler of the
cold maxims of the world, Gibbon, in Shelley's view, cannot
but clash with Rousseau, the hierophant of an unapprehended
inspiration.

Shelley's letter abounds in instances in which imagination
and reality, poetry and history, stand opposed to each other.
There is, first of all, the form of the letter, its broad architec-
tonics. At the outset Shelley announces what has been the trip's
greatest delight and what will be the major subject of his letter
—the divine imagination of Rousseau. He concludes his letter
with an extended comparison between Rousseau and Gibbon,
immediately following it with the rainbow at Lausanne and the
white houses imagined to come from Meillerie. The letter provides a terrain for a constant warfare between poetry and history. At Meillerie the fiction of *Julie* can force a French Em-
press into an attitude of reverence. At Clarens Shelley and
Byron enter into the fantasy of Julie and St. Preux's real existence only to discover that the sacred bower of the lovers has
been desecrated by a very real order of monks. Surrounded by
such a coherent reiteration of theme, a paragraph like the following assumes a greater centrality than would at first appear
from its outward disguise as digression:

On returning to the village, we sat on a wall beside the lake, looking
at some chidren who were playing at a game like ninepins. The children here appeared in an extraordinary way deformed and diseased.
Most of them were crooked, and with enlarged throats; but one little
boy had such an exquisite grace in his mien and motions, as I never
before saw equalled in a child. His countenance was beautiful for the
expression with which it overflowed. There was a mixture of pride
and gentleness in his eyes and lips, the indications of sensibility,
which his education will probably pervert to misery or seduce to
crime; but there was more of gentleness than of pride, and it seemed
that the pride was tamed from its original wildness by the habitual
exercise of milder feelings. My companion gave him a piece of
money, which he took without speaking, with a sweet smile of easy
thankfulness, and then with an unembarrassed air turned to his play.
All this might scarcely be; but the imagination surely could not fore-
bear to breathe into the most inanimate forms, some likeness of its

own visions, on such a serene and glowing evening, in this remote and romantic village, beside the calm lake that bore us hither.[35]

Shelley notes that his immediate presence at the scene of *La Nouvelle Héloïse* has helped to heighten the novel's imaginative power. But if Shelley recognizes the scenery as a useful enhancer of the imagination, he does nothing more than that. While appreciative of the reinforcement mountains and forests afford, he is scrupulously quick to assert the proper order of importance. Shelley does say, "It is inconceivable what an enchantment the scene itself lends to these delineations [i.e., of *La Nouvelle Héloïse*]." But, according to him, the novel is only getting back what it has first given. It is drawing on nothing but its own riches, for it is the novel itself "from which its [the scene's] own most touching charm arises."[36] Later on in the letter, Shelley speaks of the lake's perimeter as a terrain the primary function of which is to stimulate the imagination. To any reader of Rousseau, Meilleire and Clarens present themselves not so much to the eyes as soil and rock but "to the imagination as monuments of things that were once familiar, and of beings that were once dear to it."[37] There follows the sentence we have already quoted but which, nonetheless, seems incapable of overemphasis: "They [the dear beings of the previous quotation, i.e., the whole imagined world of *La Nouvelle Héloïse*] were created indeed by one mind, but a mind so powerfully bright as to cast a shade of falsehood on the records that are called reality."

In a note to the "Hymn to Intellectual Beauty" Mary informs us that Shelley wrote that poem as an expression of his dawning admiration for *La Nouvelle Héloïse*.[38] Even without Mary's gloss, it is obvious that in 1816 *La Nouvelle Héloïse* came upon Shelley somewhat in the manner of a theophany, a revealing of itself as both totally "other" and radically prior. Shelley's description of Rousseau's imagination as "divine" is a romantic and partially demythologized use of the word, but it is not, therefore, merely a piece of indeterminate bombast. Shelley does mean something by it, and what that is is simply ontological priority, those first things beyond the reach of such

Enlightenment figures as not only Gibbon but also that particular Jean-Jacques Rousseau who, before 1816, seems to have been the only one known to Shelley.

IV

A poetic mind, moving to the rhythms of Wordsworth, does not go far before it runs into the problem of the imagination and its relation to phenomenal nature. In the summer of 1816 Byron and Shelley met the problem together, and the event on which they sharpened their differences was the pilgrimage around Lake Geneva. Writing the third canto of *Childe Harold*, Byron in 1816 was a recent (and short-lived) convert to what he took to be the Wordsworthian religion of nature. He was a kind of fundamentalist who believed in the literal deity of sublime landscapes. When, during his long nocturnal tête-à-têtes with Shelley, he fell into opinions like the following, they must have exploded like a challenge in the mind of his interlocutor:

. . . it is the great principle of the universe, which is there [i.e., at Clarens] more condensed, but not less manifested; and of which, though knowing ourselves a part, we lose our individuality, and mingle in the beauty of the whole. —If Rousseau had never written, nor lived, the same associations would not less have belonged to such scenes. He has added to the interest of his works by their adoption; he has shown his sense of their beauty by the selection; but they have done that for him which no human being could do for them.[39]

Wordsworth's poetry celebrates the perpetual rendering and receiving that goes on between nature and imagination. When celebration gives way to analysis, the question invariably arises as to which one of these two powers is primary and which auxiliary. Byron has here awarded first place to Nature, whereas Shelley, in his letter to Peacock, goes in the opposite direction. For him, it is phenomena that dance to the tune of the human imagination, and not vice-versa.

To the two English poets the Wordsworthian context is undoubtedly the one most relevant, but it is Rousseau who has incited an argument, the importance of which he himself seems to have felt, given the nature of a passage in *Julie* to which both Byron and Shelley make precise reference.[40] The references are to part 4, letter 17, that point in the novel when Wolmar deliberately leaves his wife alone with her former lover, hoping that the latter may finally realize that what he loves exists only in his imagination—a young girl named Julie and very different from the matronly Mme de Wolmar. While out on the lake, Julie and St. Preux are caught in a storm and almost drown. They put in at the nearest beach, which happens to be Meillerie, hallowed ground to St. Preux. While waiting for the storm to subside, St. Preux persuades Julie to go for a walk. Not by chance they come to the very spot from which, several years before, the passionate young man gazed over the lake to Clarens. Then, St. Preux recalls, it was winter, and the site was desolate, and he was separated from Julie. Nevertheless, in that misery, his mind's eye was able to imagine a preternaturally radiant Julie. Now he has Julie with him and it is *la belle saison*, but these realities are a cheat, a gross falling off from his former visions: he has learned Wolmar's sobering lesson very well. Almost too well: on his way back he will be tempted to plunge both himself and Julie into a watery grave.

When St. Preux discovers that he has been worshiping a creature of his own mind and that elsewhere she no longer exists and possibly never did exist, he cries out, "Faut-il me retrouver avec toi dans les mêmes lieux, et regretter le tems que j'y passois à gémir de ton absence?"[41] Yes, Shelley would reply, because that was the time when you imagined most intensely, when the fires of your heart actually overcame the frost of winter. As Julian-Shelley says to Maddalo-Byron:

> Where is the love, beauty, and truth we seek
> But in our mind? and if we were not weak
> Should we be less in deed than in desire?[42]

Successfully manipulating a rather drab actuality, Wolmar begins the process by which he will chastise St. Preux's overheated imagination. Save for a resurgence of passion at its very end, the rest of the novel is the consequence and the somewhat ambivalent defense of this chastening. The admiration of

Shelley, however, was directed not at the reformed St. Preux but at the passionate lover, not yet subdued to Wolmar's corrective rod. Shelley never refers to any part of *Julie* subsequent to part 4, the reason for this being, I suspect, that the argument of the last two books is little else than the not totally unambiguous installation of Wolmar as the moral no less than the literal governor of Clarens. Under the influence of this decidedly "cold and unimpassioned spirit," the novel itself hardens into an icy didacticism—the expressive form for what, the last two parts make very clear, is the ideal man of the Enlightenment, whose only failing is an emotional deep-freeze that makes him unconcerned with any other god but Reason. The handing over of his novel to the Wolmar ethos must have struck Shelley not as Rousseau's ascent to judicious reasonableness but as his descent from the imaginative to the didactic, a falling out of poetry and into the "mere reason"[43] of the Enlightenment.

The vigor with which, after 1816, Shelley insisted on Rousseau as "essentially a poet" owed its force to a chronology of acquaintance and appreciation which, while it began with enlightened ideas on diet and economics, approached its end with the inclusion of Rousseau among those poets who "[had] celebrated the dominion of love, planting as it were trophies in the human mind of that sublimest victory over sensuality and force."[44] Shelley's post-1816 allusions to Rousseau all emphasize what he himself only belatedly discovered. They share, as it were, the same deep structure: "Rousseau seemingly a *philosophe*, really a poet." But drafting Rousseau into the ranks of poetry was a move complicated by the notoriety of his life, dominated as the latter had been, not by love but by peevishness, dereliction, and madness. Indeed, the most important historical given of the "Triumph of Life" is this conventional notion about the distinction in Rousseau between the brilliance of the work and the shabby egotism of the life, and Shelley's poetic variation on this theme is his not altogether confident application to Rousseau of what in the "Defence" is a much more apodictically expressed distinction between the divine poetry of love and the self-centered humans chosen to be its vehicles.

The underlying formula of the "Triumph of Life" represents an advance beyond the joyful discovery of 1816, an advance into the problematic. For the poem's formula is not the comforting one of the poet behind the *philosophe*. Rather it is the unsettling one of the poet infected by the *philosophe*, the poet sick of his civilization, struck down by a cultural malaise, the symptoms of which can scarcely be ignored in the misery-to-misery details of that mean life to which, in his egotism, the "poet" Rousseau so frantically clung and about which the world of English letters never seemed to stop writing.

In the "Triumph of Life," Shelley once again takes up the theme of *Alastor*, the distinction of the later poem being that Shelley has taken this most personal of themes—the defeat of an imaginative man—and displaced it into a specific historical context that the poem itself defines as the agent of calamity. *Alastor* suggests that misfortune is inherent to the visionary enterprise; for a similar but historic misfortune the "Triumph" would seek to find sufficient reason in a literary civilization that promotes specious and misleading notions of enlightenment. Always ready to take up a lance for poetry, Shelley was not always as sure of the matter as he liked to pretend: out of his argument with Peacock he created the magnificent rhetoric of "A Defence of Poetry"; out of an argument with himself he began but never finished the poetry of the "Triumph of Life."

5

The Breath of Darkness: A Reading of ''The Triumph of Life''

IN "THE Triumph of Life" Shelley attempted perhaps the nineteenth century's most ambitious analysis of Jean-Jacques Rousseau. One of the most baffling pieces of romantic literature, Shelley's poem is, as well, one of its most ignored masterpieces. Only recently edited from the original manuscript, it nonetheless remains a fragment, its power generally praised, its possible significance almost as generally evaded.[1] But what even T. S. Eliot has claimed for the poem—its Dantesque energy of language—is something more than mere verbal and technical facility.[2] It is the disciplined expression of a sophisticated artistic intelligence that knew what it was doing: making a statement about Jean-Jacques Rousseau.

The "Triumph" encloses a vision within a vision. Its primary visionary, whom for convenience we may call Shelley, is a citizen of Europe beset by a nightmarish swarm of great names and frantic crowds, all bound to a triumphal chariot and all leveled into a common servitude and shame. Despite Rousseau's subsequent pointing out of one distinguished personage after another, the overall effect remains that of a mob, the horror of which resides not so much in the loss of all pattern and order as in the apparent inability of anyone to be free. There is an almost complete lack of self-determination. Everyone here, it would seem, has abdicated to the horde. Confusion and aimlessness are pervasive, and when a weary and bewildered Shelley is about to ask, "Is all here amiss?" he is only becoming that which he beholds— a weary and bewildered civilization, one that has made a mess of human freedom.

Turning to Rousseau for explanation, Shelley becomes the audience for a second vision. This time it is Rousseau's autobiography, done not in the expansive narrative of the *Confessions* but in the manner of a perennial Shelley genre, the symbolically condensed life-history. Shelley's Rousseau tells his life Shelley's way, not his own. But "The Triumph of Life" is as Rousseauean in premise as it is in subject. Like the historical Rousseau, the one whom Shelley creates speaks from the conviction that for the most telling record of public events one can do no better than to turn to one's own private register of experience.

This is Rousseau's generic description of those over whom Life has triumphed:

> The Wise,
>
> The great, the unforgotten: they who wore
>   Mitres & helms & crowns, or wreathes of light,
> Signs of thought's empire over thought; their lore
>
>   Taught them not this—to know themselves; their might
> Could not repress the mutiny within,
>   And for the morn of truth they feigned, deep night
>
> Caught them ere evening.
>
> (208–215)

That he who reigns is the most abject of slaves is probably Shelley's most frequent paradox. Here, however, a new entry has appeared in his catalog of evil. In the company of the usual metonymies for the even more usual oppressors—bishops, generals, monarchs—there rather unexpectedly arrive the intellectuals, those called "the wise," those wearing "wreathes of light, / Signs of thought's empire over thought." What strategy lies behind this assimilation of thinkers to lords spiritual and temporal seems clear enough. Often enough has the power of intellect been corrupted into the deep night of dogma; often enough has *magisterium* been but the disguise and tool for *imperium*. In line with this intellectual emphasis, the generic portrait lays its stress less on political oppressions than on spiritual failures. Its one literal statement is an allusion to the Delphic oracle—"their lore /Taught them not this—to know themselves"—added to which are two parallel metaphors, one of empire, the other of light. Such exactly superimposed planes of discourse suggest their referential identity: "lore" = "might" = "morn of truth"; knowledge = conquest = enlightenment. To articulate this cluster is but to repeat one of the Enlightenment's most threadbare advertisements for itself. What Rousseau has done on his acid-tongued own is to take such received triumphalist images and then push them to a conclusion such that they turn against themselves. A handful of mutinous forces, concentrated at the capital and overthrowing a powerful but over-extended empire, is the recurrent event of a Roman Empire become decadent. Rousseau takes this sequence of disaster and turns it into a metaphor for the spiritual disarray of the European community, which has come to this pass, he suggests, because the human subject at the creative center of knowledge is one province that has remained intractable to the conquests of modern intelligence, such a neglect of inwardness being by itself sufficient to shortcircuit all would-be Enlightenment.

The assimilation of autocrat and intellectual occurs too often in the poem not to be a deliberate strategy of its author. Shelley's thinkers are consistently placed in company that is as morally incriminating as it is historically factual. Aristotle is the intellectual twin of Alexander the Great, the figure of a tyrannical jailer (268) serving for one as well as for the other. The grouping of "Voltaire /Frederick and Kant, Catherine, & Leopold" (235–236) is similarly motivated: the arch-*philosophe* of France and the magisterial professor of *Aufklärung* are as much "spoilers spoiled" as any of those eighteenth-century despots who presumed to call themselves enlightened.[3]

Even before "The Triumph of Life" Shelley had quite deliberately taken his favorite paradox of the conquerors conquered and applied it to his intellectual milieu. Analyzing the shortcomings of recent intellectual advances, he had written in "A Defence of Poetry":

The cultivation of those sciences which have enlarged the limits of the empire of man over the external world has for want of the poetical faculty proportionally circumscribed those of the internal world; and man, having enslaved the elements, remains himself a slave.[4]

The *philosophes* had told the truth, but they had not been able to tell the "whole truth."[5] Impatience with superstition, problems of method, and anxieties about clarity had led them either to ignore or to contemn the deeper and more fluid levels of consciousness, and it was precisely by his approaches to these that Rousseau distinguished himself from his age. His final work (and that which the record shows as one of the most interesting to Shelley) is *Les Rêveries d'un promeneur solitaire*, an anthology of dreamy walks on several of which Rousseau ecstatically abandons himself to what he calls "le sentiment de l'existence depouillé de toute autre affection":

Je ne médite, je ne rêve jamais plus délicieusement que quand je m'oublie moi-même. Je sens des extases, des ravissemens inexprimables à me fondre pour ainsi dire dans le systême des êtres, à m'identifier avec la nature entiére.[6]

Describing the same kind of experience, Shelley makes of it nothing less than the distinguishing characteristic of the poetic character:

Those who are subject to the state called reverie feel as if their nature were dissolved into the surrounding universe, or as if the surrounding universe were absorbed into their being. They are conscious of no distinction. And these are states which precede, or accompany, or follow an unusually intense and vivid apprehension of life.[7]

Shelley's description of reverie is perhaps less analogous with Rousseau than it is derivative from him. The relevant meanings listed in the *Oxford English Dictionary* define the naturalized English word as "a fit of abstracted musing" or "the fact,

state, or condition of being lost in thought." Shelley's definition is much more detailed than either of these. One might
even consider it technical. That the language of Shelley's
details conforms so closely with Rousseau's suggests that he
may have borrowed his description directly from the *Rêveries*.
But whatever the facts of influence may be, at least this much
may be ventured. For both Rousseau and Shelley, reverie was
a nonrational means toward "an unusually intense and vivid
apprehension of life." It was not simply a pleasant experience.
It was a way of knowing, untouched by either the neglect or the
ridicule of the enlightened.

Reverie occupies a small but quite important place in "The
Triumph of Life." An *Inferno* in miniature, the poem makes
only a few glancing allusions to a *Paradiso*, but Rousseauean
reverie is the pervasive condition of by far the most developed
of these allusions (308–331). The eschatological terms are Shelley's own: the Rousseau persona speaks of his life as a "Hell . .
. in which I wake to weep," and, by contrast, his "Heaven" is
an "oblivious spell," permeated by a

> sound which all who hear must needs forget
>
> All pleasure & all pain, all hate & love
> Which they had known before that hour of rest.
>
> (318–320)

To realize how appropriate it is that Shelley's Rousseau should
define blessedness in just such a negative fashion, one has only
to glance at the fifth promenade's celebrated analysis of reverie
as a kind of secular beatific vision, one that achieves the full-
ness of bliss only as a function of the passivity it can induce and
the experience it can, as it were, wash away:

> sans aucun autre sentiment de privation ni de jouissance, de plaisir ni
> de peine, de desir ni de crainte que celui seul de notre existence. . . .
> Tel est l'état où je me suis trouvé souvent à l'Isle de St. Pierre dans
> mes reveries solitaires, soit couché dans mon bateau que je laissois
> dériver au gré de l'eau, soit assis sur les rives du lac agité, soit ailleurs
> au bord d'une belle riviére ou d'un ruisseau murmurant sur le
> gravier. . . . Le sentiment de l'existence depouillé de toute autre
> affection est par lui-même un sentiment précieux de contentement et

de paix qui suffiroit seul pour rendre cette existence chére et douce à qui sauroit écarter de soi toutes les impressions sensuelles et terrestres qui viennent sans cesse nous en distraire et en troubler ici bas la douceur.[8]

In direct contrast to those who would wear the "signs of thought's empire over thought," the attitude, method and goal of this Rousseau is self-effacement. But although this may be what is final and deepest in Rousseau, it is not by any means the complete story of his life and work. Rousseau is more than Shelley's idea of the poet, more than the man "subject to the state called reverie." Shelley himself knew this, and indeed it was precisely Rousseau's prototypical complexity that made him an appropriate focus for Shelley's own gropings after the meaning of himself and his times. For it was the nerves of a poet under the mantle of a *philosophe*—the two of them together in Rousseau—which fired the narcissistic imagination of Shelley. Like Rousseau but with much more trust and youthful good will, Shelley had himself tried to be a worthy son of the Enlightenment, only to discover a mutiny within, which he shared with Rousseau and for the handling of which the career of the latter might well serve as guide, example, and warning.

II

Complementing Rousseau's acerbic notice of modern thinkers yoked to modern tyrants is his insistence that he alone had been innocent of collaboration. "I," says Rousseau, "was overcome / By my own heart alone"—a claim to a uniqueness and purity of disaster which the spatial dispositions of the "Triumph" confirm. For in this macabre progress poem, Rousseau is indeed unique: he sits by the wayside.

"The Triumph of Life" is a very political poem, but in it Shelley is party to neither of the polarized English factions of the post-Napoleonic era. Instead, by performing two strategic maneuvers (one within the other), he has defined his own, very individual position. His sustained metaphor of enlightenment as conquest has drafted the *philosophes* into the ranks of those

motivated and traduced by power, but simultaneous with this
rather large and potentially reactionary assimilation is the
sharp distinction he draws between the author of the *Rêveries*
and all other eighteenth-century luminaries.

On one side of the poem's starkly drawn line of division,
there hurtles the mob of the would-be powerful—not only
Napoleon but the *philosophes* as well. On the other, there stands
or (almost literally) there vegetates the lonely figure of Jean-
Jacques. Such antithetical stationing contributes to the historical specificity of a poem in which philosophical grief about
general contraries is nonetheless presented as a response to the
very immediate spectacle of Napoleon in chains:

> I felt my cheek
> Alter to see the great form pass away
> Whose grasp had left the giant world so weak
>
> That every pigmy kicked it as it lay—
> And much I grieved to think how power & will
> In opposition rule our mortal day—
>
> And why God made irreconcilable
> Good & the means of good.
>
> (224–231)

The grasping French emperor is an obvious representative of
the power contrary. As a representative of the opposed contrary, symmetry suggests Rousseau. Prior to the narrator's
lament, he is the only other historical personage to be sketched
at any length. Indeed, to place Rousseau in such an antagonis-
tic relation to Napoleon is merely to acquiesce in the conventional notion (which Shelley never seems to have questioned
and which Byron shared) that Rousseau was the inspiration of
the French Revolution and Napoleon its betrayer. As far back
as the summer of 1816, Shelley saw Rousseau as one both
responsible for and corrupted by the adventures of Napoleon.
On the site of *La Nouvelle Héloïse* he had written a tribute to that
Rousseauean "democracy" of feeling "which [Napoleon's]
dynasty outraged, and of which it was however, in some sort,
the representative among the nations of the earth."[9]

In Shelley's eyes, Napoleon did indeed betray the benign impulse on which he rode to power, but to identify that impulse with the Enlightenment would be to gloss over the distinctiveness of agony which the "Triumph" confers on Rousseau. If one takes as seriously as Shelley did the following two propositions—that Rousseau was an oddity among his intellectual peers, and that nonetheless "c'est . . . lui qui a été la cause de la révolution"[10]—then one should begin to suspect that the energy Napoleon exploited was, in Shelley's mind, something other than what is ordinarily understood as the Enlightenment ethos. As conceived by Shelley, that betrayed energy was, instead, a pathos—unique to Rousseau and as alien to the reigning values of the Enlightenment as Rousseau himself was oafish in the *salons* of its "wise and great."

What the "Triumph" assumes is explicit in a "A Defence of Poetry," where Shelley vigorously insists that the Enlightenment was not enough. Guided by its lights, Europe had seen a revolution turn into a terror and its savior into a vulgar *Imperator*. Shelley's association of Bonapartist legions and Enlightenment thought is not meant to question either the necessity of the critical intelligence or the desirability of social reform. Instead, he wishes by its fruits to question the adequacy of "mere reason" as an exclusive instrumentality toward this end. In the figure of Jean-Jacques Rousseau as he appears in "The Triumph of Life," this issue is posited within the Enlightenment itself and at a level Shelley always took to be primary—that is, the orientation and dynamics of consciousness. For, in his ecstatic reveries, Rousseau, at least momentarily, repudiated the aggressive mental activity so typical of his contemporaries. Behind the "Triumph's" description of Rousseau as an outsider, there lies the simple historical fact of the *Rêveries*—Rousseau's documentation of an eccentric penchant for the self-effacements of a solitary walker. It is this and not the entire Enlightenment that the poem identifies as the contrary of the Napoleonic power.

What Shelley sees as characteristic of Rousseauean reverie is its obliteration of the lines ordinarily drawn up between the perceiving subject and the object perceived, what in more current parlance one might call the dissolution of ego-consciousness. Taking one completely out of one's self, "reverie" denotes the absolutized form of that state of consciousness, the external operation of which is usually described in Shelley's empiricist diction as the sympathetic imagination. According to Shelley in the "Defence":

> The great secret of morals is love, or a going out of our own nature and an identification of ourselves with the beautiful which exists in thought, action, or person, not our own. A man, to be greatly good, must imagine intensely and comprehensively; he must put himself in the place of another and of many others; the pains and pleasures of his species must become his own. The great instrument of moral good is the imagination.[11]

In this peculiar blend of the psychological and the ethical, reverie would seem to function almost as if it were the sign of election and the means of revelation. Both Rousseau and Shelley were secular reinterpreters of the language of religious experience, and for both of them reverie became a kind of psychological *summum bonum*. Reverie is a state, says Shelley, and his description suggests that what he expected of it—"an unusually intense and vivid apprehension of life"—was scarcely less than what several centuries before Dante had expressed in his own, more orthodox, language of the "state of grace."

As the aggressions of Napoleon are a metonymy for "power" and the "means of good," so too the reveries of Rousseau are a complementary metonymy for "good" and "will." The two figures give historical specificity to a clash of contraries to be found not only in Shelley's "Triumph" and Yeats's "Second Coming" but also (and seminally) in the final taunt of the furies in *Prometheus Unbound*:

> The good want power but to weep barren tears.
> The powerful goodness want: worse need for them.
> The wise want love; and those who love want wisdom;
> And all best things are thus confused to ill.

Wanting power "but to weep barren tears," Shelley's Rousseau represents not simply the "good," but the apparent impotence of that good. He is that stock Jean-Jacques who had become almost an emblem of moral weakness. For, granted all the sideline fierceness of Rousseau's tongue, granted all those verbal sparks—his "words among mankind"—that lit a "thousand beacons," the literary fact remains that in Shelley's poem Rousseau just sits there in limp disengagement, his uniqueness of station dramatizing not only his vaunted purity but also the apparent ineffectiveness of that purity, its retreat from the historical realities of power and revolution that, in the eyes of almost everyone, Rousseau himself had brought to pass.

Just as Shelley's Napoleon incarnates a raw power that has betrayed the impulse from which it supposedly springs, so too his Rousseau suggests a goodness of intent, never quite capable of mobilizing itself into deed.[12] Using a symbolic shorthand of shadow, solitude, flower, and song (461–463), the Rousseau of "The Triumph of Life" catalogs what should have kept someone like him out of the path of the onrushing chariot. But all of this personal potential is to no effect because

> among
> The thickest billows of the living storm
> I plunged, and bared my bosom to the clime
> Of that cold light, whose airs too soon deform.
>
> (465–468)

Describing Rousseau's fall from grace, these lines are nothing more, and nothing less, than an English imitation of the language repeatedly used by Rousseau himself when the latter would return to his most insistent and painful image of himself as a good man not strong enough against the force of circumstance, a former innocent now damned in the sophisticated Babylon of Enlightenment Paris. Separated from Julie, St. Preux describes himself in Paris as "me voila tout-à-fait dans le torrent."[13] Speaking in his own voice about his own unfortunate initiation, Rousseau is wont to use a similar imagery of

torrent or *tourbillon*. His gift for self-dramatization is nowhere
more skillfully employed than in these repeated and elaborate
laments over that fateful turning point in his life when,
forsaking the peaceful repose of the provinces, he plunged into
a new world of theatre, café, and drawing room. In the *Rêveries*
he speaks of himself as having been "jetté . . . dans le
tourbillon du monde."[14] In the *Confessions* he is "jetté malgré
moi dans le monde sans en avoir le ton."[15] Shelley's Rousseau
similarly enters a dance "which I had well forborne" (189).
The leaders of this dance—alternately described as a "living
storm" and a "clime of . . . cold light"—are the brilliant
intellectuals of eighteenth-century France. For a symbol meant
to express the inadequacies of "mere reason," the Parisian
"scene" of icy cognition and frantic sociability provided Shelley with just the right compound of elements. Furthermore, the
misery suffered there by Rousseau epitomized for Shelley a
rather personal anxiety—the plight of the imaginative man in
an unimaginative age.

III

It is within his heart that Shelley's Rousseau locates his distinction from his *philosophe* colleagues:

> For in the battle Life & they did wage
>   She remained conqueror—I was overcome
> By my own heart alone, which neither age
>
>   Nor tears nor infamy nor now the tomb
> Could temper to its object.
>
> (239–243)

These lines admit of at least two readings.[16] In one "heart" is
taken as the antecedent of "its object" and Rousseau is understood to be lamenting over something beneficial that he has not
allowed the miseries of human life to do for him and his heart.
This is perplexingly out of character, and to unperplex us it has
been suggested that in this clause Rousseau is not lamenting at
all but rather bragging about how he has *not* succumbed in the

inglorious manner of the notables at whom he points an accusing finger.[17] In this alternate reading, first proposed by Bradley, "its object" refers to the nefarious purposes of life as pursued by her agents who are age, tears, infamy, and the tomb. (To be sure, Life herself is feminine and her agents plural, but the *neither . . . nor* construction, in which the agents are listed, divides a grammatical subject into discrete alternatives, the proximate of which ("tomb") is the determinant of subsequent number and gender: thus the correctness of "*its* object" even if tomb were not thrown into relief by the disjunctive "now" that precedes it.) The clause's multiple subject is its rhetorical center of emphasis, and what Rousseau does with this emphasis is list not indignities from which he has failed to take a chastening cue but rather adversities against which he has held firm. Grammatically a negative assertion about himself, Rousseau's clause has as its rhetorical target the conquerors conquered.

The Bodleian manuscript reveals that before hitting on "temper," Shelley wrote "model," a word more stringent in its implied accusation as to how others have allowed their energies to be confined and blocked.[18] Substituted for "model," "temper" can mean the capitulation Shelley's Rousseau wants either it or "model" to mean. But as a word prominent in the poetry of his Italian period, Shelley usually has "temper" mean something quite different from submission. It is one of his most common words (and images) for love and well being. Sometimes the word is part of an explicitly musical metaphor as when, in the joyful sunrise of the "Triumph," bird song is described as "tempering" itself to the "Ocean's orison" (7-8). At other times, it implies the perhaps more primary image of a fusing heat within which the right two metals may become stronger together than apart. Such being the habitual place of "temper" in Shelley's poetic lexicon, its function as substituted here for "model" would seem to be that of ironic deflection. It is a verbal fulcrum. With it Shelley can suggest just where Rousseau has failed even as the latter keeps insisting on just where he has stood fast.

What Rousseau means to say is that he did not capitulate to Life. Even if one accepts this claim, one cannot help but notice the arrogant and boastful tone in which it is made, and if one further recalls the hackneyed criticism of Rousseau as intemperate, one might well begin to wonder whether Rousseau's stiff-hearted egotism could temper itself to anything. The poet of the sympathetic imagination, Rousseau was, nonetheless, one of its most inept practitioners, a colossus of egotism whose botched attempts at communion with other human beings were a public and longstanding joke. The emphatic negatives with which Shelley arms this notorious misanthrope are, then, a double-edged sword with which he makes him self-inflict the most apposite of cricitisms—egotism. "My own heart alone" is the phrase of neither the most temperate nor the most loving of men.

Two of the "Triumph's" four instances of "temper" (8, 277) use the word in a technical musical sense, meaning "to tune" or "to bring into harmony." Harold Bloom has asserted that the poem is a battle of competing lights and the visions these lights inform.[19] One may add that the battle is waged on an acoustic and choreographic front no less than a visual. Its participants make their allegiances manifest through the kinds of dances they allow themselves to perform. Falling by the wayside, Rousseau has said a final no to the triumphal procession, the "dance, which I had well foreborne," but this does not insure his proficiency in some more appropriate dance of the spirit. Set apart from his rationalist contemporaries, Jean-Jacques never was able to sustain an alternative style. Fitful in opposition, he failed to fall into graceful step with a different drummer.

The identity of the different drummer within the poem must at first appear obvious. Almost all of Shelley's major works contain a feminine figure very much like the "shape all light" in the "Triumph." The appearance of this figure is a rather consistent signal that a poem's protagonist is about to approach some affective and imaginative zenith. All but one of Shelley's visionary ladies would seem to enjoy this unambiguous good character. The exception is the variant that appears in "The

Triumph of Life." Since one cannot deny the resemblance to other benign feminine shapes in Shelley's poetry, her detracters draw attention not to what this feminine figure seems but to what she does. Reminding us that Rousseau's downfall comes immediately after his meeting with her, they insist that "devils come disguised as angels . . . when they mean to tempt rather than to frighten us."[20] They contend that when she has Rousseau where she wants him, the "shape all light" destroys him:

> And still her feet, no less than the sweet tune
> To which they moved, seemed as they moved, to blot
> The thoughts of him who gazed on them, & soon
>
> All that was seemed as if it had been not,
> As if the gazer's mind was strewn beneath
> Her feet like embers, & she, thought by thought,
>
> Trampled its fires into the dust of death.
>
> (382–388)

"Trampling" and "dance of death" are, to be sure, the language of anxiety, but it is not at all certain that such panic is the proper response to what is happening. Note the cerebral narrowness with which Rousseau chooses to talk about himself. A disembodied consciousness, he presents himself as nothing but a mind and its thoughts. The word "thought," indeed, is repeated no less than three times lest one forget the eccentric devaluation it has suffered in the poem. In the introduction the narrator's insomniac "thoughts" (21) are finally laid asleep so that a "Vision" (40) may be rolled onto his brain. Thereafter, throughout its 548 lines, the poem scarcely once deviates from an anatomy of consciousness according to which the waking possessions of the mind are referred to as "thoughts" and sharply opposed to the darkly brilliant intimations of dream, reverie, and vision. The sinister "signs of thought's empire over thought" (211) are not to be confused with "the sparks with which Heaven once lit Rousseau's spirit." Aristotelianism was "throned in new thoughts of men" (267), its eventual overthrow brought about by the insurrectionary spirit (269) of Bacon, leaping "like lightening out of darkness" (270).

Confronted with the blotting action of the shape all light, Rousseau remains more attached to clear and distinct ideas than the poem in which he finds himself. For while the "Triumph" may concede clarity to be the original virtue of intellectual crystal, it is the poem's persistent emphasis that obscurantism—the immoveable opacity of rock—is its descendant as idea and cold, all-knowing egotism its legacy as temperament. Out of a perception that established paradigms may tyrannize as effectively as established religions, Shelley constructs his own paradigm for the play of the mind in his civilization, and it is to Francis Bacon that he assigns the role of Promethean liberator, that mythical Bacon of the "Triumph" who first explodes his way through the prison walls of Aristotelian system and then, matching protean mind to protean Nature "[compels it] . . . To wake and to unbar the caves that [hold] / The treasures of the secrets of its reign" (270–273). The prime intellectual virtue here is not clarity but an openness, which is both empirical and intuitive. Its historical context is the growing nineteenth-century awareness that a misplaced insistence on clarity had often acted to the same effect as the religionist's claim to know the unknowable.

With admirable historical accuracy, Shelley has Rousseau the man-thinker perceive as a threat what Rousseau the poet of the *Rêveries* celebrates. Gliding over a musical stream, the dancing lady "blots" the "thoughts" of a frightened Rousseau, and "soon," he laments, "all that was seemed as if it had been not." To be compared with this, however, is the way Shelley's Rousseau has already described his imagined "Heaven," the *genius loci* of which is the same musical stream, placed at the dawn of life:

> Thou wouldst forget thus vainly to deplore
>
>> Ills, which if ills, can find no cure from thee,
>> The thought of which no other sleep will quell
>> Nor other music blot from memory—
>
> So sweet & deep is the oblivious spell.

(327–331)

Stream and lady both turn off "thoughts" (in the former case, explicitly painful), and to each Rousseau applies an identical language—"sweet," "tune," music, "blot," oblivion. But if Rousseau speaks with rapture about the effects of the stream, it is with terror that he recoils from the dancing feet of the lady. A fearful rationalist, he trembles before a devil of destruction when he should be welcoming what he himself has described as an angel of deliverance.

Rousseau is one of the privileged few who, in Shelley's words, are "subject to the state called reverie." But, this is a gift insufficiently developed by him, an unused talent. Very early in the poem's pageant of folly and misery the narrator cryptically alludes to a similar waste of available energies:

> And weary with vain toil & faint for thirst
> Heard not the fountains whose melodious dew
>
> Out of their mossy cells forever burst
> Nor felt the breeze which from the forest told
> Of grassy paths, & wood lawns interspersed
>
> With overarching elms & caverns cold,
> And violet banks where sweet dreams brood, but they
> Pursued their serious folly as of old.
>
> (66–73)

These fountains are salutary in the same musical way as the Lethe-like stream of Rousseau's heaven. Coming after a long and belittling description of "vain toil" and "serious folly," they promise a similar release from ego. However wretched the participants of the narrator's vision may be, there does exist an alternative, and the second appearance of healing waters—that which occurs at the beginning of Rousseau's autobiography— associates this alternative with the ego-dissolving properties of reverie, the psychological precondition of love. The water music to which the dancing lady moves is, then, no less than its third appearance. But Rousseau fails to recognize the "shape all light" as another salutary and melodious fluidity. Instead, she strikes him only as a threatening "blot." This is why Rousseau too has been forced into Life's triumph. Not that he has never heard a different tune. Rather he has failed to temper himself to it, failed to recognize the lady's dance as identical with the waters of life—"the fountains whose melodious dew / Out of their mossy cells forever burst."

IV

The effect of the "shape all light" would seem to be the precise opposite of her nature. "All light" she may be, but what she does to Rousseau is to bring on a darkness described by the latter in elaborate and awestruck detail:

> All that was seemed as if it had been not,
>   As if the gazer's mind was strewn beneath
> Her feet like embers, & she, thought by thought,
>
>   Trampled its fires into the dust of death,
> As Day upon the threshold of the east
>   Treads out the lamps of night, until the breath
>
> Of darkness reillumines even the least
>   Of heaven's living eyes,
>
> (385–392)

The lady dousing Rousseau's mental fires is compared to daylight extinguishing the stars. One simile to clarify another might seem sufficient explanation. But a prolix Rousseau (or an even more notoriously prolix Shelley?) goes on to explain the daylight simile: what Day does, we are told, is prevent "the breath of darkness" from reillumining "the least of heaven's living eyes." But surely this way of looking at the Day's destruction of a starlit night is less a lament over light lost than a recognition of darkness's power to bring forth a light greater than that which the common sun sheds on the common earth; and such praise of darkness must seem odd to any reader who can still remember that this run of figurative language began with Rousseau's frightened response to imminent mental blackout.

"Lamps of night" and "heaven's living eyes" are Rousseau's two names for the same thing—stars. Proximate phrases laying claim to the same referent, they quarrel with each other almost as if meant to illustrate Wittgenstein's dictum that the bearer of a name is not its meaning. For the meaning here is nowhere else than in the protean kenning that Rousseau performs on stars—the shifts of diction by which he attempts to put them to work for his own purposes. Named "lamps of night," the stars of Rousseau's simile are very properly put out by Day: such lamps are a mere makeshift to get one through the night; the light of the sun leaves them without purpose. Betrayed by his own simile, Rousseau rephrases it so as to justify his attachment to his "thoughts." His new name for stars—"heaven's living eyes"—is, to be sure, properly exalted. So stated, the situation justifies his annoyance that Day obliterates stars or that the lady stamps out his thoughts. The rub is that these stars of vision live on the "breath of darkness," and this is what Rousseau was complaining about in the first place.

If Rousseau's language celebrates a climactic "breath of darkness," why then, on the brink of his own personal entry into darkness, should he recoil in terror? Why indeed, particularly when one recalls that at the beginning of his autobiography Rousseau so appreciatively describes an "oblivious spell"? Talking himself into self-rebuttal, Rousseau is a victim of dramatic irony. The tightly spun web of his imagery testifies to his poetic nature. Unraveled, it is a mockery of his rationalist anxieties.

And yet, the opening of the poem is a celebration of that felicity to which the morning sun seems to call the entirety of the natural world. Aside even from any confusions specific to the poem's use of light imagery, it does seem peculiar that such a calamitous action as that which the "Triumph" imitates should be introduced by a full-throated hymn of praise such as the following:

> Swift as a spirit hastening to his task
>   Of glory & of good, the Sun sprang forth
> Rejoicing in his splendour, & the mask

Of darkness fell from the awakened Earth.
The smokeless altars of the mountain snows
    Flamed above crimson clouds, & at the birth

Of light, the Ocean's orison arose
    To which the birds tempered their matin lay.
All flowers in field or forest which unclose

    Their trembling eyelids to the kiss of day,
Swinging their censers in the element,
    With orient incense lit by the new ray

Burned slow & inconsumably, & sent
    Their odorous sighs up to the smiling air.

                                                                  (1–14)

But even here there is someone not quite at home: Shelley himself. Shortly before thrusting himself into the foreground of the
landscape, Shelley changes the tune of this largely celebrative
description, bringing it to a close on the following monosyllabic
and rather sinister note of cosmogony:

    all things that in them wear
The form & character of moral mould
    [did] Rise as the Sun their father rose, to bear

    Their portion of the toil which he of old
    Took as his own & then imposed on them.

                                                                  (16–20)

Shelley may sing the praises of the sun, but his reported actions
go on to speak another language:

    But I, whom thoughts which must remain untold

    Had kept as wakeful as the stars that gem
The cone of night, now they were laid asleep,
    Stretched my faint limbs beneath the hoary stem

    Which an old chestnut flug athwart the steep
    Of a green Apennine.

                                                                  (21–26)

The sole human agent in the landscape, Shelley chooses the
unseasonable hour of sunrise to fall into his "strange trance."

He acts at 180 degrees of variance from the course of nature, his distinction being of course consciousness—the "thoughts which must remain untold / [and which keep him] as wakeful as the stars that gem / The cone of night." Pursuing his perversity even further, the narrator goes on to describe the onset of his trance as if it were the dawn of a "vision." He turns away from the reality of the sunrise only to retrieve its image as a metaphor for inward dawnings: "I knew / That I had felt the freshness of that dawn / . . . Under the self-same bough" (33–37). But the narrator's sun of vision rises only as his stars of "thought" are turned off. Vision rolls onto that mind only which has first put a stop to its ordinary waking activity. Quarreling with the Enlightenment, Shelley will not be maneuvered into the role of a barbarian cursing the light. Instead he asserts the existence of a light-revealing darkness that ordinarily is obstructed by the glare of "mere reason." And as the outward image for just such an assertion about the human imagination, Shelley has ready to hand one of the most important elements in his poetic cosmos: the perception that, as much as sunlight is indeed light, it is also an atmospheric veil blocking us off from a different, a stellar light. Still serviceable, the image of sunrise must nonetheless be liberated from the rationalist embrace. In the opening lines of the "Triumph," therefore, Shelley appropriates for himself this hackneyed self-image of the Enlightenment and turns it into a metaphor for his own very different notion of what a human dawn should be like; and indeed the major aim of the poem is to argue that the latter holds a superior claim to the image, that it is the "*true* Sun" (292).

Toward this end Shelley amplifies precisely those details of the sunrise image which one would be most wise to choose as a natural icon for spiritual imperatives. His sustained portrayal of nature as if it were in liturgical attendance upon the sun— the ocean's orison, the birds tempering their matin lay, the censer-like flowers sending "their odorous sighs up to the smiling air"—is as little orthodox romantic nature worship as it is orthodox religion. What Shelley is doing with this very stylized nature poetry is not gaping at a landscape but shaping a metaphor for the human attitude that ought to be the sun of a human life. The very first line of the poem is a clue to this effect. It is a simile that pretends to clarify the sun springing forth by comparing it to a "[swift] spirit hastening to his task / Of glory & of good." Reversing the usual spirit-to-matter direction of figurative language,[21] Shelley is performing the strategic rhetorical move by which one assumes what one wishes to inculcate. For the odd direction of his simile assumes that the physical world governed and sustained by the sun is less immediate to the poem's audience than the human world of significance and value.

The troubled Shelley of the introduction, however, does not seem to be totally free of the conventional confusions between lights natural and lights human. An enthusiastic celebrant of the sun, he is not himself fully aware of his subversive and sustaining allegiance to the breath of darkness. He seems more to grieve over his estrangement from natural light than to appreciate its implications.

"The Triumph of Life" contains only one objective incident —Shelley's encounter with his historical imagination as manifested to him in the details of the vision. If Shelley had ever completed the poem, he would probably have made his narrator-surrogate progress through the vision to a new perspective on his initial situation. Such a poetic strategy is identical with that generally at work in the genre to which "The Triumph of Life" belongs—the medieval dream-vision, an English example of which is Chaucer's "Book of the Duchess."[22] The typical narrator of the genre first gives us a rather matter-of-fact account of his approach to sleep. Subsequently dozing off, he dreams in such a way as to reveal a significance of some kind inhering in the material so jejunely perceived at the outset. A completed "Triumph of Life" was, I suspect, intended to describe a similar circle. The opening lines of the poem contain all the images necessary for enlightenment, but like the "stars / That gem the cone of night," they are lying about in a scramble. It is the vision's task to rearrange the pieces so that we may have the equivalent in lyric poetry of a recognition scene in drama.[23]

One other source for Shelley's introduction serves to establish the direction of this recognition. Falling into visionary experience, Shelley's narrator describes his physical situation in this manner:

> before me fled
> The night; behind me rose the day; the Deep
>
> Was at my feet & Heaven above my head.
>
> (26–28)

This is a virtually literal translation of lines Faust utters in one of his more vigorous flights beyond the earthly *Meer des Irrtums*. The scene is sunset when Faust exclaims:

> Doch scheint die Göttin [the sun] endlich wegzusinken;
> Allein der neue Trieb erwacht,
> Ich eile fort, ihr ew'ges Licht zu trinken,
> *Vor mir den Tag und hinter mir die Nacht,*
> *Den Himmel über mir und unter mir die Wellen.*
> Ein schöner Traum, indessen sie entweicht.
> Ach! zu des Geistes Flügeln wird so leicht
> Kein körperlicher Flügel sich gesellen.[24]

G. M. Matthews has pointed to this borrowing from *Faust*, but he does not remark that Shelley has tampered with Goethe's lines.[25] For the narrator of "The Triumph of Life," when he assumes his most oracular style, looks not toward the day but toward the night. Unlike Goethe's intellectual overreacher, the vectors of Shelley's attention point toward the night rather than the sun. That Shelley conceals this maneuver within overt praise of the risen sun suggests that he is well aware of the poem's central paradox of light and darkness, as well aware of it, one might say, as he is of the difference in perspective between Goethe's lines and his own; and the way Shelley reverses *Faust* suggests that the resolution of the paradox would take one away from the certainties of intellect and toward the intuitions of vision, away from the glare of sunlight and toward "the breath / Of darkness [which] reillumines even the least / Of heaven's living eyes." In short, "The Triumph of Life" is a more extensive treatment of that "negative capability," so succinctly explained by John Keats: "When a man is capable of being in uncertainties, mysteries, doubts, without any irritable searching after fact and reason—[the opposite of someone who] would let go a fine isolated verisimilitude caught from the Penetralium of mystery, from being incapable of remaining content with half-knowledge."[26]

Shelley's Rousseau is an ironic study in *chiaroscuro*. Trembling lest the lady trample out the light of his mind, he acts like a hoarder of that light. His language, however, spins out beyond his control, climactically rising into praise of the darkness that is behind brilliance. His retentive miscues revealed by nothing so sharply as his own words, the Rousseau persona is a literary victim constantly under the knife of Shelley's irony, and as the principal communicant and beneficiary of the sacrifice, Shelley has introduced himself into the poem. The autobiography he has manufactured for Rousseau is a cautionary tale lest he too make the same mistake, lest he too fail to realize all that is implied by what remains his stance throughout the vision—that is, his back toward the sun, his face toward the retreating night.

Because of his confusions about light and dark, Rousseau fixes the lady in a description that, to the extent that it is fearful, is correspondingly ugly. The darkening fluidity she induces he can see and describe only as a "blot." That the consequences of their meeting are as ghastly as Rousseau's language is pejorative is not a puzzle but a congruity. Things will become worse not because the lady is bad but because Rousseau so badly receives her. Rousseau's attitude determines the action of his autobiography no less than its diction.

Shelley's questing poets invariably approach their visionary ladies as if, amid the ardors of their response, they might shortly dissolve. Even if only tricked into believing the "shape all light" to be his "epipsyche," Rousseau ought likewise to respond in the heated accents Shelley's words could usually conjure. But this a frightened but still cool Rousseau does not do. Instead he plays the role of an inquisitor, peremptorily demanding of the lady, "Shew whence I came, and where I am, and why" (398). One could scarcely frame questions more ultimate than these, but they are questions the internal contradiction of which must prohibit any answer. Rousseau wants both ultimates and self, but, as the *Rêveries* should have made clear, these are incompatible desires. To reach the *sentiment pur de l'existence*, had not Rousseau himself been required to become something of a master in the art of self-destruction? The irony is as patent as the egotism of its victim was notorious: it is from the "realm without a name" that Rousseau desires an exhaustive identification of that man denominated as Jean-Jacques Rousseau, but, a fortiori, any such self-conscious ego is as alien to this kingdom as the name with which it would like to announce itself.

Pursuing what he thinks to be knowledge of self, Rousseau rises to drink from the lady's cup, his description of himself at this point being given in a language that reprises the flower imagery of the introductory sunrise: Rousseau "rising" to the summons of the shape all light is, in his own words, "a shut lily, stricken by the wand / Of dewy morning's vital alchemy" (401–402). But here again Rousseau is wiser in his similes than in his actions. He may end his cross-examination with an image of himself as an exfoliating lily, but Rousseau the man remains to make just words of Rousseau the poet, and the cross-examination remains a cross-examination.

Rousseau drinks from the lady's nepenthe, and immediately his mind becomes like a beach from which a wave has just erased the track of a deer, thus allowing a new vision to appear as suddenly as the tracks of a pursuing wolf who "leaves his stamp visibly upon the shore / Until the second [wave] bursts" (409–410). An alchemy of sorts has been accomplished, but its result has been a baser rather than a richer metal. It has generally been assumed that this obviously unattractive image of Rousseau's mind as a wolf-haunted, Labradorean desert is meant to dramatize the deadly effects of the lady's cordial. But this image for Rousseau's mind is not the effect of evil. It is its cause. Its picture of the brain as a cold desert upon the surface of which foreign impressions will "take" is a deliberately sinister parody of the epistemological image at the base of eighteenth-century rationalism. It is the Lockean notion of the mind as a tabula rasa, its cold starkness a function of the questions with which Rousseau has assaulted the shape all light.

The crisis of the poem is that moment when Rousseau drinks from the lady's cup, but the nature of this crisis becomes clear only in the subsequent lines in which the old vision gives way to the new. These lines state in extremely sharp focus the central conflict of the poem between two adversary images of consciousness. On the one hand, there is an image of the mind as a blank slab upon which discrete impressions make distinct marks. On the other hand, there is that image of consciousness developed in Rousseau's elaborate description of the retreating shape. The comparison of the disappearing "shape all light" to Lucifer's fadeout at dawn is rather too long to be simply decorative (412–433). This would be so even if the morning star were not the most important and most constant symbol in Shelley's poetry, what Yeats described as Shelley's "star of infinite desire."[27] Having identified the morning star as a symbol of highest aspiration, one may then notice how exhaustively Rousseau describes the *manner* of her continuing influence:

> And the fair shape waned in the coming light
> As veil by veil the silent splendour drops
>   From Lucifer, amid the chrysolite
>
> Of sunrise ere it strike the mountain tops—
>   And as the presence of that fairest planet
> Although unseen is felt by one who hopes
>
> That his day's path may end as he began it
> In that star's smile, whose light is like the scent
>   Of a jonquil when evening breezes fan it,
>
> Or the soft note in which his dear lament
>   The Brescian shepherd breathes, or the caress
> That turned his weary slumber to content.—
>
> So knew I in that light's severe excess
> The presence of that shape which on the stream
>   Moved, as I moved along the wilderness,

> More dimly than a day appearing dream,
>> The ghost of a forgotten form of sleep,
> A light from Heaven whose half extinguished beam
>
>> Through the sick day in which we wake to weep
> Glimmers, forever sought, forever lost. —
> So did that shape its obscure tenour keep
>>   (412–432)

Indeed, *how* her signal may continue to reach him is Rousseau's major subject. The heretofore visual image of the "shape all light" is now imagined as dispersing itself into a series of alternatives, each one of them describing the same blurred passage from visual clarity into felt obscurities, each one of them charting a synesthetic descent of light as either odor, sound or touch. The shape all light becomes a presence that "although unseen is felt," while in the adversary image the wolf leaves "his stamp *visibly* upon the shore." That the wolf track is so pointedly "visible" and the "star of infinite desire" so elaborately dim should inhibit one's prejudice against darkness, and the climactic allusion to the shape's provenance as

> A light from Heaven whose half extinguished beam
>
>> Through the sick day in which we wake to weep
> Glimmers, forever sought, forever lost
>>   (429–431)

provides the reader with an indication of value as unambiguous as the wolf in the alternative mind-image.

The misfortune of Rousseau results neither from the shape's supposed malevolence nor from her dimness of communication but rather from Rousseau's own perverse attempt to force that "obscure tenour" into something unlike itself, something more definite and precise. As an extension of Rousseau, the new vision's bright car similarly "forbids shadow to fall from leaf or stone" (445). But the events of the poem unfold in utter disregard of this prohibition:

>   the grove
>
> Grew dense with shadows to its inmost covers,
>> The earth was grey with phantoms, & the air
> Was peopled with dim forms, as when there hovers

> A flock of vampire-bats before the glare
> Of the tropic sun, bringing ere evening
> Strange night upon some Indian isle
>
> (480–486)

The concluding simile places familiar Gothic horrors against an unusual and heightening background of tropic glare. A strange and premature night has descended on the well-lit life of Rousseau, and the language used to describe his predicament is similar to his own critique of the reputedly "wise": "for the morn of truth they feigned, deep night / Caught them ere evening."

That Shelley plots a dawn-to-nightmare trajectory both for the wise and for Rousseau is no accident. For in "The Triumph of Life" Shelley is not writing simply about one individual. He is using that individual as a type for the mind of an entire era, and in the disappointments of the (axiomatically Rousseauean) French Revolution he has a symbolic language ready to hand: lines 495–515 catalog the return in new ghastliness of the various political, social, and sexual tyrannies the abolition of which had been the professed and conscious aim of the new order. In Shelley's view the failure of the French Revolution was a consequence of the Enlightenment's shallow understanding,[28] and such grotesqueries as populate the latter part of this, his last poem, are his final condensations for a post-Revolutionary time of dereliction and dismay. The subject of the poem is, therefore, both individual and typical, both personal and historical. Personally, it records the fall from grace which Rousseau habitually discerned in his life and always situated at precisely that moment when, he would have us believe, he involuntarily became a member of the Parisian intelligentsia. Historically, the poem assumes the commonplace that Rousseau is to be placed at the imaginative source of the French Revolution and then goes on to describe the failure of the revolution as a consequence of Rousseau's prototypical apostacy from imaginative vision: "want of the poetical faculty" is Shelley's autopsy on abortive revolution.[29]

V

"The Triumph of Life" is a history of Rousseau's energies and their Urizenic curtailment. That which is curtailed is love and the sympathetic imagination; that which curtails them is egotism and pride of intellect. Rousseau himself had previously dealt with this theme. His monodrama *Pygmalion* defines imaginative energy precisely as a going out of oneself brought about through the agency of "céleste Vénus, par qui tout se conserve et se reproduit sans cesse": the protagonist's statue comes to life only when he is finally able to say, "il me suffira de vivre en elle."[30] Love and imaginative realization are thus identified, and it is Pygmalion's anxieties about self which alone delay, as it were, the birth of Galatea. But here, once again, the actions of Rousseau's art are not necessarily the experience of his life. For *Pygmalion* is in the nature of a compensatory wish fulfillment. In it, self is overcome and the imagination liberated because, one strongly suspects, in its author's life the former had been so tyrannical and the latter so checked.

I bring up *Pygmalion* for more than the relevance of its theme. The fact is that Shelley almost certainly read this work and almost contemporaneously with his composition of "The Triumph of Life." A translation appeared in the May 10, 1820 issue of Leigh Hunt's *Indicator*, a periodical Shelley read with no little regularity.[31] In a brief introduction Hunt remarks how Rousseau's Pygmalion seems to fall in love with his own creation "almost out of vanity."[32] He goes on to assert that Rousseau "was a kind of Pygmalion himself . . . perpetually yet hopelessly endeavouring to realize the dreams of his imagination . . . Pygmalion's self predominates over the idea of his mistress, because the author's self pressed upon him while he wrote."[33] Hunt concludes with a personal criticism of Rousseau which may have suggested to his friend why *Pygmalion* was a triumph of realized creativity but the actuality of its author a catastrophe of crippled imagination:

The only actual difference between the fabulous solitary and the real one, was, unfortunately, that Pygmalion seems to have been willing enough to be contented, had he found a mistress that deserved him; whereas Rousseau, when he was really beloved, and even thought himself so, was sure to be made the ruin of his own comfort; partly by a distrustful morbidity of temperament, and partly perhaps by *a fastidious metaphysical subtlety, which turned his eye with a painful sharpness* upon the defects instead of humanities of his fellow creatures.[34] [emphasis added]

The case of Shelley's Rousseau is the same: an intellect too quick to meddle with the mistress of imagination.

Goethe's *Faust* is another representation of man and his feminine ideal which was very much in the forefront of Shelley's mind at this time. Furthermore, his discussion of *Faust* occurs in very close and suggestive association with the same archetype as it appears in *La Nouvelle Héloïse*. Writing to John Gisborne on April 10, 1822, Shelley waxed enthusiastic about the etchings with which Friedrich A. M. Retzsch had illustrated Goethe:[35]

What etchings those are! . . . Margaret in the summer house with Faust!—The artist makes one envy his happiness that he can sketch such things with calmness, which I dared only to look upon once, & which made my brain swim round only to touch the leaf on the opposite side of which I knew that it was figured.[36]

Shelley's interest in the summer house scene is to be expected, for the meeting of Faust and Margaret is identical in kind with his own obsessively recreated scenes of man and feminine ideal. More instructive perhaps are the links Shelley forges between himself, Goethe, and Rousseau. Asking Gisborne to recall a letter from *La Nouvelle Héloïse* ("L'Amant de Julie dans le cabinet de sa Maitresse. Ses transports en l'attendant."), Shelley asserts that the *Faust* etching is "an idealism"[37] of this letter, the *style haletant* of which features Rousseau as man of feeling and recalls very strongly the heat of similar scenes in Shelley.[38]

But of all these scenes crowding upon Shelley's attention, only Rousseau's *Pygmalion* ends with love triumphant; and to Shelley, no less than to Leigh Hunt, such a happy denouement must have appeared as merely the fond wish of its author. Truer to the sad reality of things was the way in which love was frustrated in both *Faust* and *La Nouvelle Héloïse*. Rousseau's novel may begin with St. Preux's fire, but it ends in an avalanche of homiletic ice about the reasonable way things are done at the Clarens of Madame de Wolmar, wife, *chatelaîne*, and mother. Nor does the Faust-Gretchen match quite work out either. Thomas Mann's comment would be pertinent here, even if *Faust* were not a major source of "The Triumph of Life": "Faust became guilty before Gretchen . . . her story is the tragedy of intellect becoming mortally guilty to beauty."[39]

The plot of *La Nouvelle Héloïse* is spiritual *fiasco*, the latter a word the French have adapted from the Italian that they might have a specialized term for episodes of sexual impotence. The love affair with which *La Nouvelle Héloïse* begins it checks through the will of the two principals. St. Preux, Rousseau's surrogate, shrinks from intimacy with Julie even as he maintains daily contact with her. If Julie is the new Eloise, St. Preux is left with the now edifying part of Abelard—self-mutilation. The action of "The Triumph of Life" is also spiritual *fiasco*. Invited into the presence of the shape all light, Rousseau is unable either to enjoy or to retain it.

The *Confessions* contain one rather long account of a very literal *fiasco*, an incident trivial in itself but one which Rousseau insists is profoundly revelatory. He describes how, upon entering the bedroom of a courtesan, "comme dans le sanctuaire de l'amour," he is suddenly struck with the horror that this good and generous "chef-d'oeuvre de la nature et de l'amour" is a "misérable coureuse livrée au public." This reflection causes Jean-Jacques to sit down and cry. Naturally Zulietta is taken aback and must be reassured. However, no sooner has Rousseau done this than he notices that she has

un téton borgne. Je me frappe, j'éxamine, je crois voir que ce téton n'est pas conformé comme l'autre. Me voila cherchant dans ma tête comment on peut avoir un téton borgne, et persuadé que cela tenoit à quelque notable vice naturel, à force de tourner et retourner cette idée, je vis clair comme le jour que dans la plus charmante personne dont je pusse me former l'image, je ne tenois dans mes bras qu'une espéce de monstre, le rebut de la nature, des hommes, et de l'amour.

Unable to conceal either his discovery or his anguish, Rousseau finds he has offended Zulietta, who coldly tells him: "*Zanetto, lascia le Donne, e studia la matematica.*"[40]

Since Rousseau has said that with this one incident "vous allez connoitre à plein J. J. Rousseau," suffice it to say that it is Rousseau's head that is the agency of frustration. Rousseau himself knows this. Those unwilling to credit him with a sense of humor should study carefully the great discovery of the missing nipple, for Rousseau's language here mimics the very rhythms of intellectual discovery: *je me frappe, j'examine, je crois voir,* and so on for several lines. Zulietta herself knows it: *lascia le Donne, e studia la matematica* is inspired in the precision with which it sums up what has happened. Even Leigh Hunt seems to know it. According to him Rousseau "was sure to be made the ruin of his own comfort . . . by a fastidious metaphysical subtlety, which turned his eye with a painful sharpness upon the defects instead of the humanities of his fellow creatures."

I do not wish nor am I able to claim that this incident from the *Confessions* is source and model for the botched encounter of the "Triumph." Shelley almost certainly read the *Confessions.* He has left us some general remarks about them, but in these remarks he never singles out this scene as, for example, he singles out St. Preux in Julie's bedroom or the summerhouse scene in *Faust.* Nevertheless, Rousseau himself does rather insistently label the scene as one of total self-recognition: "Qui que vous soyez qui voulez connoitre un homme, osez lire les deux ou trois pages qui suivent vous allez connoitre à plein J. J. Rousseau."[41] Such a rhetorical fanfare demands that one read Rousseau in a way scarcely foreign to Shelley and the other heirs of Wordsworth. It demands that one see within the individual and the ordinary what might be general as truth and extraordinary as revelation. Shelley certainly could have become that kind of reader.

Be all this as it may, I have discovered no factual or documentary link between Shelley and this specific episode of the

Confessions, and the extent of my claim can only be that the intelligible content of Rousesau's self-revelation is identical with the analysis of Rousseau given in "The Triumph of Life." Trying to characterize Rousseau, Shelley could have done worse than to take a hint from the self-recognitions of the man himself. Indeed the manner in which Rousseau introduces the *fiasco* reads almost as if it were a note for the conduct of Shelley's Rousseau before the "shape all light":

Jamais si douce jouissance ne s'offrit au coeur et aux sens d'un mortel. Ah du moins, si je l'avois su gouter pleine et entiére un seul moment! . . . . . . [Rousseau's ellipses] Je la goutai, mais sans charme. J'en émoussai toutes les délices, je les tuai comme à plaisir. Non, la nature ne m'a point fait pour jouir. Elle a mis dans ma mauvaise tete le poison de ce bonheur inéfable, dont elle a mis l'appetit dans mon coeur.[42]

In "The Triumph of Life" Rousseau's head likewise poisons the gifts of his heart. The difference is that Shelley's poem places responsibility for this not on a "nature" that has made one incapable of sexual pleasure but on a cultural and intellectual situation that has made one incapable of Shelleyan flights. Shelley's Rousseau acts in a very unShelleyan manner in a very Shelleyan situation, the "Triumph's" "clime . . . of cold light" being too frigid not so much for Rousseau's Zulietta as for one of Shelley's own visionary women. The climate of the "Triumph" is a cultural climate. It is what we now call the Enlightenment. Contingent upon human action, it influences Shelley's protagonist in the shape not of biological fate but of recent intellectual history.

To Shelley the Enlightenment was incapable of arriving at that "whole truth"[43] to which (he implied) it laid claim. As his final symbol for such proud inadequacy, Shelley chose the brilliant but sinister juggernaut of the "Triumph," an image into which he could condense all his suspicions about an intellectual movement perhaps as destructive in consequence as it had been imperial in presence.

First described as a "cold glare . . . icy cold," the chariot is then caught in the net of yet another of Shelley's epic similes:

> Like the young moon
>
> When on the sunlit limits of the night
> Her white shell trembles amid crimson air
>   And whilst the sleeping tempest gathers might
>
> Doth, as a herald of its coming, bear
> The ghost of her dead Mother, whose dim form
> Bends in dark ether from her infant's chair,
>
> So came a chariot on the silent storm
> Of its own rushing splendour, and a Shape
>   So sate within as one whom years deform
>
> Beneath a dusky hood & double cape
> Crouching within the shadow of a tomb,
> And o'er what seemed the head, a cloud like crape,
>
> Was bent a dun & faint etherial gloom
> Tempering the light.
>
>   (79–93)

The new moon is an egg-like "shell," whose carrying of the old moon forebodes a tempest that is described in infant-like terms as sleeping and gathering might.[44] As herald of the approaching storm, the new moon is said to "bear" the "dim form," and the latter is indeed all that one may imagine as gestating within its crescent. One month hence she will give birth to nothing but an identical gloom. It is that and only that toward which the egg-like shell is waxing.

What Shelley's lunar imagery describes is not an objective cycle. It is, rather, something quite different and quite subjective. For all of this—metaphoric tenor as well as vehicle, chariot as well as moon—exists only as the shared vision of Shelley and Rousseau. The chariot exists not as fact but as an image projected out from the developing condition first of Shelley and then of Rousseau. And what is most noteworthy about this image as it appears in Rousseau's symbolic autobiography is the timing of its arrival: it is permitted to enter on the scene only after the "shape all light" has exited (434 ff.). Usurping the latter's place at the poem's center of interest, the chariot is identical in function with the "desert Labrador,"

Shelley's disenchanted model of the Lockean mind. The moon-chariot image represents not life itself but life as perceived by a certain kind of mind, life as seen in a certain light.

A chiaroscuro of icy glare and infernal darkness, the moon-chariot is a precise iconographic analogue for the continually reprised narrative sequence of the poem from light to nightmare. Caught in the stasis of poetic simile, the juggernaut reveals itself with a completeness and precision ordinarily blurred by its hurtling motion. Once arrested in this way, the triumphal pride of the chariot is recognized for what it is—an appropriately spectral frontispiece to the gloomy events Rousseau will go on to describe as occurring under its auspices. The shape of things to come in the poem, the image is likewise the completed form of what in history began so gloriously as an appeal to Reason.

When Shelley takes the intellect—which the poem usually represents as the glare of the sun—and stamps on it the insignia of the moon, he is guilty of neither astronomical nor poetic confusion. In Shelley's view, an accurate iconography of human faculties required a drastic revision of the compliment the Enlightenment never tired of paying to itself. It required, namely, that the sun of intellect "[bursting] through the clouds of bigotry that obscured the moral day of Europe"[45] be demoted into a subordinate rank. Now such a subordinate rank is the distinguishing chracteristic of the moon: earth's cold satellite can give off only so much light as it is able to reflect from the sun. And furthermore, it is precisely in this way—as a disparaging symbol for intellect—that Shelley often used the moon image, most notably in *Epipsychidion*.[46] For the "Triumph of Life" initially to affix sun imagery to the Enlightenment is simply to recognize a metaphoric situation that stands in need of revolution; for it then to substitute the moon for the sun is to try to enact that revolution in the mind of its audience. The driver of the moon-chariot is both a literal and a moral incompetent. Literally, he cannot see the winged shapes that draw his chariot. Figuratively, he can neither fathom nor govern the springs of his own action. Totally derivative in motion, he fails to see what is primary, and in his pride would seem to pretend

that he is himself equal to that distinction. He thinks his moon
a sun.

All of this is made clear by the glancing reference made to
the "wonder-winged team" drawing the juggernaut:

> upon the chariot's beam
> A Janus-visaged Shadow did assume
>
> The guidance of that wonder-winged team.
> The Shapes which drew it in thick lightnings
> Were lost: I heard alone on the air's soft stream
>
> The music of their ever moving wings.
> All the four faces of that charioteer
> Had their eyes banded . . . little profit brings
>
> Speed in the van & blindness in the rear,
> Nor then avail the beams that quench the Sun
> Or that his banded eyes could pierce the sphere
>
> Of all that is, has been, or will be done.—
> So ill was the car guided.
>
> (93–105)

The point of all this is not, as Harold Bloom has contended,
that the chariot is an infernal parody of divine self-propulsion.[47]
Obviously there is a team of some kind providing the power for
the chariot. But it is no more visible to its would-be driver than
to Shelley, and so the motion of the chariot is rough and anarchic, the path it cuts a chaotic jumble. The reference to the
unseen team—"I heard alone on the air's soft stream / The
music of their ever moving wings,"—is, by contrast, strikingly
mellifluous and airy. These lines—as tactile as they are audi-
tory—fly out from a surrounding texture of sound which clogs
the verse with monosyllables much as the chariot itself obscures
with "thick lightnings" the shapes that draw it. The conflicting
elements of the visual image are thus paralleled by those of its
spoken performance. The outcome along one track, however,
is the opposite of that along the other: through the chariot's
thick lightnings the visual shapes have no way of penetrating;
through the densities of the verse "the music of their ever moving wings" does find a way to Shelley's ear. The "*silent* storm

[of] rushing splendour,'' the message conveyed on an invisible ''soft stream'' of air—this pointed antithesis is a clue to the attenuated manner in which alone we may expect alphas of energy to become present to us.

The contrast thus established between an obscuring light and a communicated ''soft stream'' of music is but one instance of a larger strategy evident within the poem—the sustained mischief of its play on the imageries of sight, sound, and touch. In ''The Triumph of Life'' glare would seem to be king, a lighting effect that acts as a physical metaphor for the pyrrhic victory of Enlightenment values. If Europe must *see* in order to believe, Europe can expect nothing more than the ''shape without the grace of life''—that is, the stark grotesqueries of the poem's final section. But behind such immediately garish display, the poem asks less to be seen than to be heard and felt, for it is only by making such demands that it may remain true to its nature as an audacious satire of the Enlightenment, its tyrannies and usurpations. The clarity of the visual image may be the idol of some poets and more critics, but for Shelley it would not serve. It was precisely this poetic and conceptual piety he was seeking to dethrone, and the imageries of feeling and sound as well as those of motion and odor provided him with a subversive vantage point from which he might success-fully mock the reign of clarity within which a rationalist ethos too easily assumed that its light was the most appropriate image both for the savor of wisdom and for the motions of grace.[48]

Shelley's thematic use of visual imagery explains why the chariot of triumph is perceived almost exclusively as light, a light the excess of which is withering—''a cold glare . . . icy cold.'' It also explains why she whose place the glare usurps—the ''shape all light''—disappears to sight but quite pointedly not to any of the other senses. Light imagery dominates in the poem, but it is consistently ironic. So imperially does the char-iot shine that it ''(forbids) shadow to fall from leaf or stone''; so insolently does the poem disregard this prohibition that (anticipating Freud's ''return of the repressed'') it deals there-after with nothing but spectres, hobgoblins, and grotesques.[49]

VI

The glare of the chariot is a "severe excess" while the fading "shape all light" is said to be "from Heaven" and so soft that it is experienced only as a "caress" or a "scent" or a "breath." Glare is Shelley's characteristically more energetic analogue for the Wordsworthian "light of common day," and as in Wordsworth so too in Shelley: another kind of light does exist, but caught in the glare, it cannot be seen but only, as it were, barometrically felt. Even on an overcast day the sun continues to choreograph a dance of air currents; Shelley's "true sun" of human experience is a similar *Deus absconditus*, pervasive in its influence but manifest only as breath—an obscure *spiritus*.

How Shelley characterizes darkness as a kinesis symbolic of human desire may be clarified by once again examining the morning star simile for the retreating "shape all light," lines 411–432. For an action conventionally described in images of descent, the figure employs instead a language of ascent. The "shape all light" does not drop out of sight. Rather she transcends the visual and epistemological ken of Rousseau, a rather large notion, to be sure, but one very precisely represented in Shelley's most basic image of the world: daylight as a stratum of atmospheric veils whose nourishing enfolding of the earth is likewise a literal circumscription of its perceptual field.[50] The atmospheric veils of light are not, however, the totality of the envelope in which earth travels through space. Equally present both in fact and in Shelley's poetry is the "cone of night." The Shelleyan macrocosm begins, therefore, with the earth and its surrounding sphere of (obscuring) light, into which is wedged a nocturnal conic section, its apex located at the outer rim of the atmospheric sphere. If this is, as well, the Shelleyan microcosm, then the most revealing detail about the cone of night is that its arrowlike configuration thrusts upward beyond the veils of daylight and toward the firmament. Shelley's astronomical conceit not only impugns daylight as obscurantist; it also makes a complementary suggestion: that darkness is a revelatory impetus, a gathering energy targeted so as to pierce the limiting dome of air.

But Shelley is not content with representing merely a static cone of night. Instead he writes of the cone of night not as a being but as a becoming, not as a place of darkness but as an energy of light, and it is his image of the morning star which allows him to do this. For that star derives it name from the fact that at a certain time during the year its light will persist even until daylight has dispelled the last and inmost trace of darkness. From earth, therefore, the star will appear to be located at precisely that mathematical point that is the apex of the cone of night. Encroached upon by daylight, the light from the star will give the appearance of spiraling inward toward a final invisibility. It is this choreography of a waning star which Shelley exploits in order that he may speak of darkness dissipating as if it were a light retreating. Time after time in his poetry, the path of retreating night is made visible only as the locus of this Luciferean light. Night rushing westward becomes for him a diminishing cone, the radius of which finally contracts into the lasar-like pulse of the morning star. (The *locus classicus* of this is the following from "To a Skylark":

> Keen as are the arrows
> Of that silver sphere,
> Whose intense lamp narrows
> In the white dawn clear
> Until we hardly see—we feel that it is there.)

Poised at the cone's apex, the star is that radiance toward which darkness thrusts. The image suggests, indeed, that darkness is less a substance than it is a movement or an energy—a mounting pressure marshaling itself into a needlepoint of penetration. Darkness is *spiritus*, and thrusting through veils is the action by which it defines itself.

The morning star is, of course, the planet Venus. Available as an astronomical conceit, the planet of love is that one light— "forever sought, forever lost"—under which Shelley metaphorically subsumes almost all of the evanescent feminine ideals of his poems. The goddess of beauty, Venus animates every Shelleyan hero, but typically Shelley speaks of her not as beauty but as love. A Humean sceptic, he presents this putative ultimate not as she might be in herself but only as she makes her effect on mankind. The perhaps imaginary form toward which human energies strain, she is "known" only as she is plotted by those energies, interior tropisms that may minister to the sense as lightly (and as powerfully) as "a caress [that turns] weary slumber to content." As Aphrodite, then, the morning star is a veiled figure; it is only as Eros that she manifests herself—that demonic energy described by Socrates as the offspring of the plenty of visionary beauty and the poverty of real limitation.

At daybreak night recedes toward the "star of infinite desire," the latter seeming to draw darkness along with it beyond the veils of our atmosphere. Now, since Venus is also the evening star, one may imagine night's descent as the same process in reverse: beginning as Venus-Hesperus' penetration of the atmospheric veils, night dilates downward into a benediction of darkness from this, the "true Sun." And such is in fact what the Rousseau of Shelley's poem does imagine. Having lost the morning star within the glare of daylight, he "hopes / That his day's path may end as he began it / In that star's smile" (417–419). As Professor Glenn O'Malley has pointed out, Shelley's use of the Lucifer-Hesperus image is very stylized.[51] It is one time of year when Venus appears as the morning star, another when she appears as the evening star. Shelley, however, has placed the two at either extremity of a single "Day," a span of light clearly meant to represent the span of a human life. The point is that Shelley appropriates for his "true sun" the same course over a lifetime that the natural sun runs over a daytime.

Rousseau's hopes for the second coming of love soon turn to conviction as with evident assent he thus summarizes the good news of a love-guided Dante:

> How all things are transfigured, except Love;
> For deaf as is a sea which wrath makes hoary

> The world can hear not the sweet notes that move
> The sphere whose light is melody to lovers

(476–479)

An affirmation of the abiding music of love, these lines lay even more stress upon the assertion that the "world" is tone-deaf to the performance. Occluded during our "day," Venus continues to play, but her "sweet notes" reach ears most of which are deaf and hearts most of which remain unmoved. No longer fully present to us, she leaves only the most tenuous of traces. No longer a substantial here and now, she becomes the wraiths of memory and desire, a blessedness past and a blessedness future. The image for the former is the morning star fleeting away beyond the veils of daylight; the image for the latter is the night's promise of Hesperus. The two are, of course, one— as are the "sacred few" (128–134), so clearly divided into the eagles of the dawn and the sacrificial victims of the dusk, "they of Athens & Jerusalem" who "put aside the diadem / Of earthly thrones or gems, till the last one / Were there."

"The Triumph of Life" is an effort to represent life as most fundamentally a kinetic energy. If the poem is to be an effective analogue for such a world, then it must embody similar energies. The opening lines, for example—"*Swift* as a spirit *hastening* to his task / Of glory and of good the Sun *sprang* forth" (emphasis added)—should ultimately reveal themselves as performed in a language that while most immediately about enlightenment, is more fundamentally a prototypical instance of energy thrusting itself into manifest being. They are lines more imitative of a process than of a product. They are not so much about light as about the "*birth* of light."

Once apprised of this kinetic element in Shelley's poetry, one cannot help noticing how especially mobile is the world Shelley creates for "The Triumph of Life."[52] The poem's basic assumption is that life is most appropriately imagined as movement along a path. The first description of the conquered has them "hurrying to and fro." The young in that procession are frenetic, while the old are ambulatory grotesques who "Shake their grey hair in the insulting wind, / Limp in the dance &

strain with limbs decayed'' (166–167). More specifically: it is stated that Bacon "[Leapt] like lightning out of darkness" in order to elucidate a nature which is itself described as a Protean energy (269–273); Rousseau himself sees life as "Figures ever new / [Rising] on the bubble" (248–249); and when the narrator in turn describes Rousseau as like an "old root which grew / To strange distortion" (182–183), we have what is ordinarily conceived statically as shape described instead as the action of growing, such slight deviations from the normal way of seeing things being typical of the kinetic bias of Shelley's imagination. It would seem, then, that the Socratic "know thyself," about which the poem is so insistent, is more specifically the insistence that one know and sense oneself as essentially an energy of desire rather than a stasis of consciousness.

Read with even a minimal sensitivity to the kinetic, such typically "fuzzy" Shelleyan locutions as the "enamoured air" of line 39 should begin to appear what they almost always are: intelligibly motivated; holistically integrated into the language of the poem; firmly rooted in the very foundations of Western literary and philosophical tradition. The "glory and the good" toward which the Spirit-Sun springs is simply Shelley's translation of τὸ καλὸν καὶ τὸ ἀγαθόν toward which the Platonic Eros is impelled. The air has become alive with light and activity precisely because of the spirit-like eros of the sun which the kinesis of the opening lines does not so much describe as recreate. The flowers that elsewhere in the introduction "unclose / Their trembling eyelids to the kiss of day" need not, therefore, be reduced to a muted Shelleyan shriek. They are, instead, a rather precise image for the way in which Plato's *Symposium* argues desire to be generative of life.

Describing the Sun of the "Triumph" as if it were a creative Eros, Shelley characterizes the air caught up in its wake as "enamoured," a word which, later on in the poem Shelley will attribute to Rousseau himself. Trying to describe his prelapsarian experience of the "shape all light," Rousseau puts it this way:

> As one enamoured is upborne in dream
> O'er lily-paven lakes mid silver mist

To wondrous music, so this shape might seem

Partly to tread the waves with feet which kist
The dancing foam, partly to glide along
The airs that roughened the moist amethyst.

(367-372)

In "kist / The dancing foam" each word counts: "kist" reprises the introduction's "kiss of day" and is similarly energizing; "foam" is ἀφρός (the folk etymology for "Aphrodite" which Hesiod raised to a fixed poetic truth);[53] the dance of the foam is the barometric trace and signature of the goddess. The "partly . . . partly" construction embodies the Socratic definition of love as a demonic energy the two poles of which are earth and heaven.

Stylistically as well as ontologically "The Triumph of Life" is a world of becoming rather than one of being. Its life is made up not of things but of acts, not of nouns but of verbs. The life of Rousseau himself begins as an influx of energy: "In the April prime / When all the forest tops began to burn / With kindling green, touched by the azure clime / Of the young year" (308-311). Reminiscent of the opening motivation for Chaucer's Canterbury pilgrims—"So priketh hem Nature in hir corages"—these lines imitate an identical energy: that of *Venus genetrix*. The poem's introductory lines suggest that their subject is both an archetypal "birth of light" and that historical birth of light known as the European Enlightenment, an intellectual movement whose constant claim was that it had made "the mask of darkness [fall] from the awakened earth." Indeed, the subject of these lines is the disparity between the archetype and the specific, their strategy being satiric incongruity and their desired result the perception that the Enlightenment did not entirely deserve the name it had given itself. The lines' most concrete referent, the Enlightenment is nonetheless mocked by a presentation of light so much more insistent than itself about the voluntarist origins of illumination.

The root of Enlightenment disabilities is its shortsightedness, its myopic insensitivity to the energies that underlie every human construction, not excluding the cognitive. The "Defence of Poetry" is explicit about this:

> While the sceptic destroys gross superstitions, let him spare to deface, as some of the French writers have defaced, the eternal truths charactered upon the imaginations of men. . . .
>
> The exertions of Locke, Hume, Gibbon, Voltaire, Rousseau, *(Shelley's note: "I follow the classification adopted by the author of the *Four Ages of Poetry*. Although Rousseau has been thus classed, he was essentially a poet. The others, even Voltaire, were mere reasoners.") and their disciples, in favor of oppressed and deluded humanity, are entitled to the gratitude of mankind. Yet it is easy to calculate the degree of moral and intellectual improvement which the world would have exhibited, had they never lived. . . . But it exceeds all imagination to conceive what would have been the moral condition of the world if neither Dante, Petrarch, Boccaccio, Chaucer, Shakespeare, Calderon, Lord Bacon, nor Milton, had ever existed; if Raphael and Michael Angelo had never been born; if the Hebrew poetry had never been translated; if a revival of the study of Greek literature had never taken place; if no monuments of ancient sculpture had been handed down to us; and if the poetry of the religion of the ancient world had been extinguished together with its belief. The human mind could never, except by the intervention of these excitements, have been awakened to the invention of the grosser sciences and that application of analytical reasoning to the aberrations of society which it is now attempted to exalt over the direct expression of the inventive and creative faculty itself.[54]

VII

Donald Reiman has speculated that the "Triumph's" final reference to a "happy . . . fold" (547) is an allusion to the same evening star in whose light Rousseau hopes to end his life:

> In his late poetry Shelley more and more frequently drew upon the Christian metaphor of the sheepfold as a symbol of human salvation, usually using in conjunction the symbol of Venus as Hesperus, the evening star, which, appearing when the shepherd led his sheep to the fold at the end of day, Milton had called the 'folding-star' [*Comus*, 93] . . . . Thus Rousseau's declaration beginning "Happy those for whom the fold" might have continued with an affirmative use of

'fold' as the sheepfold into which were gathered followers of the 'folding-star' of Love.[55]

Stripped of any suggestion of Christian orthodoxy, this would indeed seem to be the most plausible ending toward which the poem is urging itself. Rousseau, it should be recalled, has dropped out of Life's triumph. Now, at the conclusion of the fragment, he casts his eye on the retreating chariot "as if that look must be the last" (546). The poem seems about to strike out on a new movement, one that would be dominated not by the chariot of Life but by Love's folding-star, one that, in leaving behind the ethos of the Enlightenment, would define the Rousseauean genesis of revolution not as "that application of analytical reasoning to the aberrations of society [but as] the direct expression of the inventive and creative faculty itself."

In the "Triumph of Life" Shelley seeks to reverse the invidious comparison ordinarily made between Rousseau the writer and Rousseau the man. While the use to which he put this comparison may seem identical with that of many Englishmen since Burke—to belittle the would-be revelations of the writer by the calamities of the man—such is not Shelley's usual use of the distinction, and, with *Adonais* as a precedent, the evening-star imagery of the "Triumph" could very readily have been used so as to close on the uplifting note struck by the emphatic assertions of the "Defence":

Let us assume that Homer was a drunkard, that Vergil was a flatterer, that Horace was a coward, that Tasso was a madman, that Lord Bacon was a peculator, that Raphael was a libertine, that Spenser was a poet laureate. . . . Their errors have been weighed and found to have been dust in the balance; if their sins were as scarlet, they are now white as snow; they have been washed in the blood of the mediator and redeemer, Time.[56]

Allowing his Rousseau persona to perform the imaginative acts of a poet, Shelley suggests that inept Rousseau still remained one of the poetic elect. Repeatedly in "The Triumph of Life" Rousseau the inept victim is balanced by Rousseau the master of language, the forger of simile. As an example we may take Rousseau's two similes for the "shape all light."

Deliberately misty and strategically vague, they represent an approach toward the shape more appropriate than cross-examination:

> As one enamoured is upborne in dream
>   O'er lily-paven lakes mid silver mist
> To wondrous music, so this shape might seem
> . . . .
>   as on the summer evening breeze
>
> Up from the lake a shape of golden dew
>   Between two rocks, athwart the rising moon,
> Moves up the east, where eagle never flew.
>
>   (367–369, 378–381)

The effect of these similes may be vague, but it is an effect very deliberately contrived, each component of the general vagueness having been very judiciously chosen so as to bring together the major symbols of the poem. This is especially true of the second simile: the setting (insofar as anything so dynamic may be called a setting) is the dark, upward impetus of the "evening breeze"; the "shape of golden dew" reprises "shape," one of the poem's most important words, and does so as it associates the highest value with the subtlest wisps of phenomena; "between two rocks" suggests an obdurate narrowness from which the shape is escaping into larger vistas; her passage "athwart the rising moon" further specifies the sublunar existence she is transcending; "up the east" echoes the frequent allusion to the "true sun";[57] the ineligible eagle, the symbol of the Napoleonic as well as the Roman conqueror, is a final disparagement of the power contrary, a final hint as to why the revolution attributed to Rousseau was so disastrously perverted.

Shelley's rather conventional choice of Rousseau as the prototypical man of his era was not a prolegomenon to the usual strategies of counterrevolutionary propaganda. He did not set out either to question the professions of the revolution by its deeds or to stain the imagined sublimities of *Julie* by the confessed baseness of its creator. Indeed, he set out to do precisely the reverse. He took this duality of Rousseau, this "disguise [staining] that within which still disdains to wear it," and tried to make it into an optimistic emblem for times of apparent calamity but real progress. With perhaps excessive boldness, he constructed an acid test for the "Defence's" assertions about the radical distinction between man and poet. He took probably the best known and certainly the most extreme contemporary example of the distinction, and then he sat down to write a poem that would be a reclamation of Rousseau's work from the corrosive influence of his life and hence a model for the way the benign impulse of the French Revolution ought to be similarly distinguished from its pragmatic failures. There is little doubt as to what results Shelley wished to educe from this acid test. There is a great deal of doubt as to whether the "unwilling dross" of Rousseau's life did not, in the end, prove too great a resistance to such "plactic stress" as Shelley's spirit was still capable of bringing to the misery of that life and to the decadence of European liberty. Perhaps the "Triumph" is unfinished not so much because of the untimely death of its author as because a chastened Shelley could no longer either believe in or perform acts of hope like the final stanzas of *Adonais*. The self-analysis Shelley gives Rousseau—"I was overcome by my own heart alone"—is almost certainly displacement for Shelley on himself: "Love far more than hatred has been to me . . . the source of all sorts of mischief."[58] And such defects as this, Shelley may have at last been forced to concede beyond hope of repair, and unfinished as it is, the "Triumph of Life" may dramatize the kind of personal and public failures it ostensibly set out to redeem.

Postscript

ERNST CASSIRER'S *The Philosophy of the Enlightenment* is still the best comprehensive book on that intellectual and cultural movement that is the subject of "The Triumph of Life."[1] Cassirer's understanding of the Englightenment is both more accurate and more inclusive than that of Shelley. In field after field, the German philosopher and historian of ideas elucidates a historical development within which what Shelley understood as an exclusively French rationalism is *aufgehoben*—matured no less than surpassed—in the form German thought took toward the end of the eighteenth century, a form very often described as preromantic.

Shelley is a romantic in anyone's book, but his critique of Enlightenment failings is identical with Cassirer's history of Enlightenment culminations. Quoting Condillac in 1755, the latter fixes the direction according to which he will graph the subsequent movement of Enlightenment thought:

les idées renaissent par l'action même des besoins qui les ont d'abord produites. Elles forment, pour ainsi dire, dans la mémoire des tourbillons qui se multiplient comme les besoins. Chaque besoin est un centre d'où le mouvement se communique jusqu'à la circonférence. Ces tourbillons sont alternativement supérieurs les uns aux autres, selon que les besoins deviennent tour-à-tour plus violens. Tous font leurs révolutions avec une variété étonnante: ils se pressent, ils se détruisent, il s'en forme de nouveaux à mesure que les sentiments, auxquels ils doivent toute leur force, s'affoiblissent, s'eclipsent, ou qu'il s'en produit qu'on n'avoit point encore éprouvés. D'un instant à l'autre, le tourbillon qui en a entraîné plusieurs est donc englouti à son tour; et tous se confondent aussitôt que les besoins cessent: on ne voit plus qu'un chaos. Les idées passent et repassent sans ordre, ce sont des tableaux mouvans qui n'offrent que des images bizarres et imparfaites, et c'est aux besoins à les dessiner de nouveau et à les placer dans leur vrai jour.[2]

As he summarizes Condillac, Cassirer puts it very succinctly both for Shelley and for that phase of the Enlightenment Shelley failed to recognize: "The usual order of ideas, which had been reaffirmed and sanctioned by Cartesian psychology, is thus reversed. The will is not founded on the idea, but the idea on the will."[3] Coming from the pen of a French rationalist, Condillac's voluntarist enthusiasm toward *le vrai jour* is of a kind and in a voice Shelley considered unavailable to any other *philosophe* besides Rousseau. It is true that Cassirer expounds a historical synthesis within which Shelley was an engaged antithesis, but it is also true that the English poet need not have been quite as ignorant as he was. A learned and indefatigible autodidact, Shelley did not entirely escape the educational lacunae into which the self-taught commonly lead themselves. Before the summer of 1816, Shelley's Rousseau was himself little else than just another Enlightenment *prosateur*. Shelley soon righted that misconception, but he never did arrive at any generous estimate of French letters. On that subject he remained as bigoted in his way as Coleridge in his. But the action of Shelley's genius redeems the incompleteness of his facts. His presentation as criticism of that which Cassirer presents as the last turn in a historical dialectic is not so much an error as it is the condition of one who would be the hierophant of an unapprehended inspiration.

If what Shelley thinks is, according to Cassirer, the very climax of the Enlightenment, then one will have to find a name for it other than irrationalism. Actually, Shelley is arguing for nothing more than a more reasonable reason, one intelligent enough to throw such light as it can on its own nonrational genesis. Unreasonable reason seeking to engross everything to itself was what Shelley took to be the condition of the mind in his era, and in "The Triumph of Life" his purpose was the very rational one of setting limits. Purpose, however, is not achievement, and even lunatics can, for such purposes as they have, imagine reason as "thought's empire over thought." What distinguishes Shelley from such as these is the coolness and the magnitude of his formal achievement. "The Triumph of Life" imitates Dante in a way that the ear of T. S. Eliot was quick to recognize as the best of its kind in English.[4] And it is more than *terza rima* which unites Shelley to Dante. It is a basic strategy. The *Commedia* begins and ends in mystery, but it remains throughout a massive intellectual structure, a wholly self-conscious architectonic. Designed according to a similar paradox, the "Triumph" exists as an even more nervous tension between the solidity of its form and the explosiveness of its final intent. In it we have the same tightly forged tercets and the same impetus toward that which Dante's faith may imagine as both an ingathering and an efflorescence, but which Shelley's agnosticism can take no further than a simple glance outward toward the "folding star" of Venus.

A post-Enlightenment *Commedia*, the "Triumph" is not sure of its ending because it is not sure of a *paradiso*; but even of an incomplete "Triumph" one may justly say what Hippolyta says of *A Midsummer Night's Dream*: it "grows to a great constancy." The poem makes sense. The center holding, its pieces do fall into place and they do assume a shape that is all light, all intelligible. The relentless interlacing of the *terza rima* is only the most outward form of this great constancy, but it too is exploited by Shelley. The tercet of Dante exerts a continual formal pressure such that the pouncing verbs caught within its traces coil themselves into an ever more tightly sprung energy. So too with Shelley who in *Adonais* described himself as a "pard-like spirit beautiful and swift /A love in desolation masked." A barely contained energy is what both Dante and Shelley sing. Each of them situates himself in a resistant medium. Each is "Swift as a spirit hastening to his task / Of glory and of good." Each "[springs] forth, rejoicing in his splendour." And the pardlike quality of Shelley's verse is in him, no less than it is in Dante, the embodied form not for some parochial emotion but for an idea: that even while we founder in this *Meer des Irrtums*, it is still (perhaps) *l'amor che muove il sol e l'altre stelle*. When Shelley makes explicit reference to Dante, he does more than simply use the "Triumph" as a forum within which to compliment his *maestro ed autore*. In addition, he fixes an identity in argument and invites a comparison in craft. He boldly but tactfully suggests that in him Dante has found a worthy successor, one whose intellect and skill are equal to the measure of the *Commedia*:

> Behold a wonder worthy of the rhyme
>
> Of him whom from the lowest depths of Hell
> Through every Paradise & through all glory
> Love led serene, & who returned to tell
>
> In words of hate & awe that wondrous story
> How all things are transfigured, except Love;
> For deaf as is a sea which wrath makes hoary
>
> The world can hear not the sweet notes that move
> The sphere whose light is melody to lovers—
> A wonder worthy of his rhyme.
>
> (471–480)

Why formal rigor is not a virtue more commonly ascribed to Shelley is an anomaly in literary history, but one not difficult to explain. *Adonais* may serve as an example. A formal *tour de force*, it insists on ending with a leap into the dark:

> The breath whose might I have invoked in song
> Descends on me; my spirit's bark is driven,
> Far from the shore, far from the trembling throng
> Whose sails were never to the tempest given;
> The massy earth and sphered skies are riven!
> I am borne darkly, fearfully, afar;
> Whilst, burning through the inmost veil of Heaven,
> The soul of Adonais, like a star,
> Beacons from the abode where the Eternal are.

The reader may acknowledge this final stanza as indeed the ultimate outcome of the "one spirit's plastic stress," but as a literary ending it seems no more final than the words with which the "Triumph" trails off; and it is probably the very same gesture—a beckoning outward and up. For this is the very motion and shape of Shelley's later poetry: shaping inward becoming thrust outward; artistic compactness preparing visionary lift-off; plasticity reversing itself from centripetal to centrifugal. Both elements in the Witch of Atlas' boat are here—the ice of formal control, the dark fire of eros—but it has been too easy to let the fire seem to melt the ice.

Coincident with the "Triumph's" formal and intellectual rigor is its placing of itself in the profane and cluttered world of history. It has now become almost axiomatic to define *Alastor* as if it were the ur-text for Shelleyan themes of aspiration and defeat.[5] Such a characterization of the youthful work is not without its uses. Shelley's poetry does exhibit persistent themes. But more important than such constants of subject matter is the displacing (specifically the narrowing) of their sphere of operation. The poet-hero of *Alastor* is virtually a disembodied spirit, and the thinness of his context inevitably gives to his sufferings the tone of unfocused growing pains. By contrast, the "Triumph" happens in the densities of recent history. Still a visionary poet, Shelley relocates his vision and his defeat *out there* in the public world of his audience. From an adolescent mystic he transforms himself into a citizen prophet.

In 1816 Edward Gibbon may have been a whipping boy for Shelley as romantic discovering Rousseau as romantic, but that was an imbalance for which the historical densities of the "Triumph" are an obvious corrective. To Shelley Roman decadence and the blindness of modern intellect are each an instance of the conquerors conquered. He can use the stuff of one as the image for the other, a Roman triumph as the vehicle for statements about Enlightenment *hybris*. History repeats itself, and naming that which repeats is, according to Shelley, the vocation of the poet. "A poem," the "Defence" tells us, "is the image of life expressed in its eternal truth." "Eternal truth" will sound like a flight of Ariel only to one who disregards the first part of the definition, the establishment of the genus of "poem" as "image of life." For that "image of life" is meant to qualify and indeed to place such eternal truths as poetry may have to offer. It suggests that history is the only perceivable locus for these truths and that recurrence is the grammar of their existence. A poem about Greeks in 1821, a poem entitled not *Greece* but *Hellas*, is the fullest expression of this new Shelleyan perspective, this new immanence.

Shelley's romanticism is the Enlightenment's heir no less than its critic. It argues against the Enlightenment, but it does so on the latter's own ground and according to the latter's own criteria of evidence and coherence. And that for which it argues is not a parochial emotion but a public idea. One should, therefore, insist on a criticism of romanticism both more thoughtful and more elegant than simply to call it a "somewhat inelegant System of Thoughtlessness."[6] One should distrust any revaluation of Shelley which would presume to lead us into its understanding of Shelley's ignorance precisely because it remains so ignorant of Shelley's understanding.[7]

Notes

INTRODUCTION

1. Saussure, *Cours de linguistique générale*, 5th ed. (Paris, 1960), pp. 30–31. (My translations.)

2. For other modern readings of the "Triumph of Life," none of them sufficiently historical, see Harold Bloom, *Shelley's Mythmaking* (New Haven, 1959), p. 252; G. M. Matthews, "On Shelley's 'The Triumph of Life,'" *Studia Neophilologica* 34 (1962): 104–134; Donald H. Reiman, "*The Triumph of Life*": *A Critical Study* (Urbana, Ill., 1965); Neville Rogers, *Shelley at Work*, 2d ed. (Oxford, 1967), pp. 273–304; J. J. McGann, "The Secrets of an Elder Day: Shelley after *Hellas*," in *Shelley, Modern Judgements*, ed. R. B. Woodings (New York, 1968), p. 267; John A. Hodgson, "The World's Mysterious Doom: Shelley's *The Triumph of Life*," *ELH* 42 (1975): 595–622; Charles E. Robinson, *Shelley and Byron: the Snake and Eagle Wreathed in Fight* (Baltimore, 1976), pp. 221–231.

3. Voisine, *Jean-Jacques Rousseau en Angleterre à l'époque romantique* (Paris, 1956), p. 279.

4. Ibid., p. 4.

5. Ibid., p. 290.

6. The phrase comes from Ezra Pound's forty-fifth canto where, in the Annunciations depicted on church walls, "halo projects from incision"—an admirably succinct image for successful visionary art.

7. See especially Shelley's preface to the *Revolt of Islam*, a poem originally subtitled *A Vision of the Nineteenth Century*: *Poetical Works*, ed. Hutchinson (Oxford, 1960), p. 31.

8. "Poet": "Defence of Poetry," ed. John E. Jordan (New York, 1965), p. 67; "greatest man since Milton": *Letters of Percy Bysshe Shelley*, ed. Frederick L. Jones, (Oxford, 1964), 1:494.

1: ROUSSEAU'S ENGLISH REPUTATION

1. Richard B. Sewall, "Rousseau's First Discourse in England," *PMLA* 52 (September 1937): 908–911. See also bibliography of eighteenth-century English translations of Rousseau in Henri Roddier, *J.-J. Rousseau en Angleterre au XVIIIème Siècle* (Paris, 1950), pp. 397–404.

2. The preface is reproduced in William Bowyer, *Miscellaneous Tracts* (London, 1785), pp. 450-452.

3. *Monthly Review* 5 (August 1751): 237.

4. Besides Bowyer's translation there was also one published in April 1752, by Richard Wynne: see a notice in the *Gentleman's Magazine* 22 (April 1752): 195. See also bibliography in Roddier, *Rousseau en Angleterre* p. 397.

5. *A Discourse upon the Origin and Foundation of the Inequality among Mankind* (London, 1762). See Roddier's bibliography, p. 398.

6. *Oeuvres diverses,* 2 vols. (Paris, 1756).

7. *Monthly Review* 18 (January 1758): 96.

8. *The Edinburgh Review for the Year 1755,* 2d ed. (London, 1818), pp. 130-134. See also Richard B. Sewall, "Rousseau's Second Discourse in England from 1755 to 1762," *PQ* 17 (April 1938): 97-114.

9. James Boswell, *Life of Johnson,* ed. G. B. Hill, revised L. F. Powell (Oxford, 1934-1950), 1:437-443.

10. *London Chronicle,* 5 (8-10 February 1759): 138.

11. Roddier, *Rousseau en Angleterre,* p. 49.

12. *London Chronicle,* 5 (8-10 February 1759): 138-139; 5 (10-13 February 1759): 146-147; 5 (15-17 February 1759): 161-162; 5 (22-24 February 1759): 185-187; *Monthly Reivew* 20 (February 1759): 115-134. *Critical Review* 7 (January 1759): 48-59. *London Magazine* 28 (January 1759): 38-40. *Annual Register* 2 (1759): 479-484.

13. *First Discourse* (London, 1760), p. vi.

14. *Annual Register* 2 (1759): 479; *Critical Review* 7 (January 1759): 48.

15. The letter in which Voltaire's remark occured was included in both the October and November 1755 issues of the *Mercure de France,* France's most prestigious literary journal, which had some circulation in England. Furthermore, Voltaire appended this letter to the 1756 edition of his tragedy, *L'Orphelin de la Chine,* and Jean Nourse, the London bookseller specializing in French books, brought out a French edition dated 1756. The lack of interest in the second discourse is confirmed by the absence of any mention of the letter in the reviews of *L'Orphelin de la Chine* (v. *Monthly Review,* Appendix [1755], 13: 493-505) and the letter's deletion from the English translation brought out by Baldwin in 1756.

16. Charles Palissot de Montenoy, *Les Philosophes* (Paris, 1760).

17. *Monthly Review* 23 (October 1760): 318-323.

18. *Monthly Review* 23 (December 1760): 492.

19. *London Chronicle* 9 (4-7 April 1761): 336.

20. Benjamin Christie Nagle, *The Monthly Review: First Series, 1749-1789: Indexes of Contributors and Articles* (Oxford, 1934), p. 23.

21. *Monthly Review* 23 (December 1760): 492; *Critical Review* 11 (January 1761): 66.

22. *Gentleman's Magazine* 31 (January 1761): 34.

23. *Critical Review* 11 (January 1761): 65.

24. The seven are in *La Nouvelle Héloïse,* Book II: letters 14, 16, 17, 19, 21, 23, 26. Letter 14, on Parisian manners in general, was excerpted in the following: *Gentleman's Magazine* 31 (February 1761): 62-68; *London Chronicle,* 9 (23-25 April 1761): 396-397; *London Magazine* 30 (April 1761): 171-173; *Monthly Review* 25 (September 1761): 192-214.

25. *London Chronicle* 9:547–548.

26. On Clarens see *London Chronicle*: 10 (16–18 July 1761): 58–59; 10 (30 July–1 August 1761): 107–109; 10 (13–15 August 1761): 156–157; 10 (15–18 August 1761): 164–166; 10 (18–20 August 1761): 172–174; 10 (27–29 August 1761): 204; 10 (24–26 September 1761): 300–302; 10 (29 September–1 October 1761): 316–317. The only letters unconnected with Clarens that appeared in the English press were: an account of Julie's religion (Book 6, letter 8); the crisis in the conquest of St. Preux's passion and the only "passionate" piece to be reproduced in the press (4, 17); and, significantly, three separate appearances, in the *London Chronicle* (10: 339–340), the *London Magazine* (30: 469–472), and the *Monthly Review* (25: 254–260), of a laudatory letter on the manners of Geneva (5, 5).

27. *Gentleman's Magazine* 31 (September 1761): 395–397; *Scots Magazine* 23 (September 1761): 471; *London Magazine* 30 (October 1761): 536–537.

28. Ernst Cassirer, *The Question of Rousseau* (Bloomington, 1963), pp. 83–84.

29. Letter of Rousseau to M. de Franquières, dated 15 January 1769. See *Correspondance générale de Rousseau*, ed. Dufour-Plan (Paris, 1924–1934), 19:48–63. The Dufour-Plan edition of the letters is not totally satisfactory or totally reliable. But it is still standard for Rousseau's career subsequent to September 1766. Prior to this date, we have the first thirty volumes of what will be, when completed at the Taylor Institution, Oxford, the standard edition of Rousseau's correspondence: R. A. Leigh, ed., *Correspondance complète de Jean-Jacques Rousseau* (1965–1977).

Both here and elsewhere in quotations of Rousseau and his contemporaries, I reproduce the eccentric but, I assume, the historically accurate orthography of the standard editions.

30. *Critical Review* 13 (February 1762): 100.

31. *Critical Review* 14 (November 1762): 336.

32. *London Chronicle* 12 (29 June–1 July 1762): 4–5; 12 (6–8 July 1762): 27; 12 (21–23 September 1762): 291–293.

33. *London Magazine* 31 (August 1762): 404–406.

34. *Emilius and Sophia; or a New System of Education* (London, 1762).

35. *Critical Review* 15 (January 1763): 31.

36. *London Chronicle*, 11 (19–22 June 1762): 589.

37. *Monthly Review* 27 (August 1762): 152.

38. Rousseau's letter renouncing his citizenship was reproduced in the *London Chronicle* of 2–4 June 1763 (13: 533) and in the June issues of the *London Magazine* (32: 323–324) and the *Scots Magazine* (25: 350). The *London Chronicle* also printed the remonstrances on this matter addressed to the Council by the Genevan citizenry: a four-column piece on 6–8 September 1763 (14:234–235) and a five-column piece the very next issue, 8–10 September 1763 (14: 242–243).

39. *Critical Review* 13 (February 1762): 100.

40. Ibid., p. 107.

41. *London Chronicle* 12 (26–28 February 1762): 204.

42. *British Magazine* 4 (August 1763): 409.

43. Boswell, *Life of Johnson*, 1: 441.

44. Ibid., 1: 444.

45. *Critical Review* 14 (December 1762): 430.
46. *Annual Register* 5 (1762): 225.
47. As quoted in *Monthly Review* 27 (September 1762): 217.
48. Boswell, *Grand Tour*, ed. Pottle (New York, 1953) p. 235.
49. Ibid., p. 253.
50. *Monthly Reivew* 31 (December 1764 Appendix): 500.
51. D. Mornet, "L'Influence de J.-J. Rousseau au XVIIIème Siècle," *Annales de la Société Jean-Jacques Rousseau* 8 (1912): 44. For a more recent presentation of Mornet's thesis, see Joan McDonald, *Rousseau and the French Revolution: 1762–1791* (London, 1965).
52. *London Chronicle*, 11 (26–29 June 1762): 615–616.
53. Peoples, "La Querelle Rousseau-Hume," in *Annales Rousseau*, 18 (1927–1928): 1–331; Crocker, *Jean-Jacques Rousseau* (New York, 1973), pp. 265–302. See also Roddier (*Rousseau en Angleterre*, pp. 259–306) who is charitable toward Rousseau and perceptive about Hume's apparent inability correctly to gauge the behavior of such a delicate nervous system. Peoples includes the texts of the many letters on the subject that appeared in the *St. James Chronicle* of 1766 and 1767—the medium in which Rousseau's misfortunes became a protracted cause célèbre in England.
54. So far as I know, there is only one unqualified advocate for Rousseau, Henri Guillemin in *Cette affaire infernale* (Paris, 1942).
55. Letter to Hume, 10 July 1766, in *Correspondance générale*, 15: 299–324.
56. *Exposé succinct de la querelle qui s'est élevée entre David Hume et J.-J. Rousseau* (Londres [in reality Paris], 1766).
57. That the persuasion toward a complete narrative of the dispute came to Hume from across the channel is evident from the letters of his Parisian friends, conveniently brought together in an appendix to *The Letters of David Hume*, ed. Grieg, 2 vols. (Oxford, 1932), pp. 407–440.
58. *Mélanges de Voltaire*, ed. van den Heuvel (Paris, 1961), pp. 849–857.
59. Ibid., pp. 859–876.
60. Ibid., p. 875.
61. In a letter from a Genevan correspondent named Boursier, dated 30 July 1766. See Grimm, *Correspondance littéraire*, part 1, 1765–1768, 6 vols. (Paris, 1813), 5: 309. This letter is not printed in the standard Tourneux edition of the *Correspondance littéraire* (Paris, 1877–1882), presumably because it is not the work of Grimm, Diderot, or any of the other principals.
62. Rousseau, *Correspondance générale*, 17: 47.
63. James Boswell, *The Journal of a Tour to Corsica; and Memoirs of Pascal Paoli*, ed. Marchand Bishop (London, 1951), p. 49.
64. *Critical Review* 22 (December 1766): 466.
65. David Hume, *Concise Account* (London, 1766), p. 91.
66. Arthur Young, *Letters Concerning the Present State of the French Nation* (London, 1769), p. 353.
67. J. H. Magellan in de Presles and Magellan, *Relation ou notice des derniers jours de J.-J. Rousseau* (Londres, 1778), p. 24.
68. Quoted from Grimm, Diderot, et al., *Correspondance littéraire*, ed. Tourneux, 16 vols. (Paris, 1877–1882), 12: 141–142. See also *Monthly Review* 60 (February 1779): 136–143; *Gentleman's Magazine* 49 (April 1779): 174–176; *London Magazine* 48 (May 1779): 195.

69. Diderot, *Oeuvres*, eds. Assézat-Tourneux (Paris, 1875–1877), 3: 91.

70. See *Monthly Review* 60 (February 1779): 136–143; 60 (April 1779): 313–315; 61 (October 1779): 299–303.

71. Note to a new edition of James Beattie, *An Essay on the Nature and Immutability of Truth*, 4th ed. (Edinburgh, 1773). Quoted from *Scots Magazine* 35 (February 1773): p. 79.

72. *Monthly Review* 60 (February 1779): 137.

73. *Universal Magazine* 68 (May 1781): 225.

2: THE *CONFESSIONS* IN ENGLISH POLITICS

1. *Monthly Review* 66 (June 1782): 530.

2. Letter of John Gillies, dated 18 May 1782. See Albert Schinz, "La Collection Jean-Jacques Rousseau de la Bibliothèque de J. Pierpont Morgan," *Smith College Studies in Modern Languages*, 7 (October 1925–July 1926): 28–30.

3. *Critical Review* 55 (May 1783): 346.

4. *Monthly Review* 67 (September 1782): 252.

5. *New Review* 1 (June 1782): 374.

6. *Monthly Review* 66 (June 1782): 537.

7. Ibid., 69 (August 1783): 150.

8. Ibid., 66 (June 1782): 530.

9. Ibid., 67 (September 1782): 232.

10. *Analytical Review* 6 (January–April 1790): 385.

11. *Monthly Review*, n.s. 2 (August 1790): 571.

12. Ibid.

13. *Critical Review* 70 (August 1790): 202.

14. See McDonald, *Rousseau and the French Revolution*; see also Jean Roussel, *Jean-Jacques Rousseau en France après la Révolution: 1795–1830: lectures et légende* (Paris, 1972).

15. From the report of the Committee of Public Instruction delivered on 15 September 1794 (preparatory to the installation of Rousseau's ashes in the Pantheon) and printed in *Honneurs publics rendus à la mémoire de J.-J. Rousseau* (Geneva, 1878), p. 61.

16. Ibid., p. 67.

17. Ibid., pp. 69–70.

18. Decree of 18 March 1794, in *Honneurs publics*, pp. 34–35.

19. Edmund Burke, *Reflections* (New York, 1955), p. 200.

20. Resolution of 21 December 1790, in *Honneurs publics*, p. 9.

21. Edmund Burke, *Works* (Boston, 1866), 4: 25.

22. Ibid., p. 26.

23. Ibid., p. 27.

24. Ibid., p. 25.

25. Ibid., p. 26.

26. Ibid., pp. 30–31.

27. Ibid., p. 31.

28. *Oeuvres*, 1: 134.

29. *Works*, 4: 25.

30. Ibid., p. 26.

31. Ibid., pp. 27–28.

32. *Remarks on the Letter of the Rt. Hon. Edmund Burke Concerning the Revolution in France* . . ., 2d ed. containing *Remarks on Mr. Burke's Letter to a Member of the National Assembly* (London, 1791), pp. 173, 181.

33. Ibid., p. 169.

34. *Gentleman's Magazine* 63 (March 1793): 225.

35. *Universal Magazine* 102 (January 1798): 21.

36. *Edinburgh Review* 1 (October 1802): 11.

37. *Anti-Jacobin* 21 (September 1805): 477.

38. Ibid., pp. 481–482.

39. *Monthly Review*, n.s. 48 (December 1805): 364.

40. *Gentleman's Magazine* 76 (January 1806): 19.

41. *Monthly Review*, n.s. 48 (December 1805): 359.

42. *Edinburgh Review* 7 (January 1806): 377.

43. As printed in ibid., 23 (July 1814): 302.

44. All of the unflattering descriptions of Rousseau cited above are taken from excerpts selected and printed by these reviewers themselves. See *Quarterly Review* 9–11; *Edinburgh Review* 21 and 23; *Monthly Review* 72–75.

45. *Quarterly Review* 9 (March 1813): 101.

46. *Edinburgh Review* 23 (July 1814): 129.

47. Quoted in a review of Thomas Green, *Diary of a Lover of Literature*, in the *Quarterly Review* 4 (August 1810): 155–156.

48. *Quarterly Review* 8 (December 1812): 297.

49. *Monthly Review* 71 (August 1813): 468.

50. Ibid., pp. 469–470.

51. *Quarterly Review* 11 (April 1814): 174–175.

52. Ibid., pp. 175, 176.

53. *New Review* 2 (July 1782): 17.

54. Ibid., p. 24.

55. *Critical Review* 55 (May 1783): 346.

56. Ibid.

57. *Monthly Review* 69 (August 1783): 149.

58. Mme de Staël, *Oeuvres complètes*, ed. Treuttel-Wurtz (Paris, 1820 to 1821), 1: 54–55.

59. *Monthly Mirror* 8 (August 1799): 72.

60. *Monthly Review* 75 (December 1786): 565.

61. Ibid., 66 (June 1782): 539 ff.

62. *Analytical Review* 11 (December 1791): 528.

63. Mary Wollstonecraft, *A Vindication of the Rights of Women* (London, 1792), p. 45.

64. Ibid., p. 100.

65. Ibid., p. 179.

66. *Anti-Jacobin* 19 (December 1804): 462.

67. *Anti-Jacobin* 1 (July 1798): 115.

68. *Anti-Jacobin* (the weekly) 2 (9 July 1798): 627–628.

69. Thomas Jefferson Hogg, "The Life of Percy Bysshe Shelley," in *The Life of Percy Bysshe Shelley* . . . , ed. Humbert Wolfe, 1:1 to 2:158 (New York, 1933), 2: 107.

70. *Works*, 4: 24.

71. William Godwin, *Fleetwood* (London, 1805), 2: 180.

72. Ibid., p. 181.

3: ROUSSEAU AND THE MAJOR ENGLISH ROMANTICS

1. *Prose Works of William Wordsworth*, ed. Owen-Smyser (Oxford, 1974), 1: 332.

2. Hazlitt's essay on Godwin appears in his *The Spirit of the Age*, in *Complete Words*, ed. Waller-Glover (London, 1902), 4: 207.

3. *Prose of Wordsworth*, 1: 36.

4. *Prelude* (Oxford, 1959) Book 2, lines 216–217.

5. Voisine, *Rousseau en Angleterre*, pp. 203–204.

6. Ibid., p. 479.

7. Ibid., p. 207.

8. See, in addition to the "Mock on" song, Blake's "The French Revolution," ll.276–282: *Poetry and Prose of William Blake*, ed. David Erdman and Harold Bloom (New York, 1965), pp. 294–295, 468–469.

9. *A Concordance to the Writings of William Blake*, ed. David V. Erdman (Ithaca, N.Y., 1967), 2: 1596.

10. Blake, *Poetry and Prose*, pp. 198–199.

11. "William Godwin," in *The Spirit of the Age*, 4: 204–205.

12. *Collected Works of Samuel Taylor Coleridge*, ed. Kathleen Coburn (Princeton, 1969), vol. 4, *The Friend*, 2 vols., ed. Barbara E. Rooke, 2:113–114.

13. Ibid., vol. 1, *Lectures 1795 on Politics and Religion*, ed. Lewis Patton and Peter Mann, 1:160.

14. Ibid., pp. 214–229.

15. *Collected Letters of Samuel Taylor Coleridge*, ed. Earl Leslie Griggs (Oxford, 1956), 1: 214.

16. *Collected Works of Coleridge*, ed. Patton-Mann, 1: 351.

17. *Collected Letters*, 1: 245.

18. Ibid., 1: 563.

19. *Notebooks*, ed. Kathleen Coburn (Princeton, 1973), vol. 3, note to entry 3775, c. May 1810.

20. Ibid., 2: 2598, May–June, 1805.

21. Except where otherwise indicated, I shall quote from the original (1809–1810) version of the *Friend* as it appears in the second volume of Barbara E. Rooke's edition. The relevant pages of that edition are 2: 111–133. They make up numbers eight and nine of the original periodical, and their original dates of publication are respectively 5 October 1809 and 12 October 1809. In the first volume of Rooke's edition, the corresponding pages of the 1818 version are 1: 129–143 and 1: 186–202.

22. Rooke, 1: 136.

23. Ibid., p. 136n.

24. *Collected Works of Coleridge, Lay Sermons*, ed. R. J. White, 6:74–77. Written in 1816, these general condemnations of Jacobinism in the *Statesman's Manual* are to be compared with a letter of Coleridge's, written two years later and containing, as his last extended reference to Rousseau, the insistence to a conservative friend that he had been a mocking critic of Rousseau for no less than two decades (*Collected Letters*, 4: 880). When, as Coleridge tells it, he

showed his unkept garden to a still unreconstructed Rousseauist, he used its degradation as the text for the following sermon, delivered on the spot in 1797: "NAY! BUT HEAR ME BEFORE YOU CONDEMN. I intended to educate it strictly on the ROUSSEAU PLAN, and to have preserved it from all artificial Semination—but I don't know how—the beasts from Hell, or the winds of chance have filled it chockful with Nettles, Hensbane, Nightshade, Devil's bit, Fools'-parsley, and (taking up the plant [*Rhinanthus Cristagalli*] as I looked steadfastly at him) COXCOMBS, Citizen John!" The moral is clear: Coleridge's Rousseau is the staple of caricature, the natural man down on all fours but still driven by vanity; to follow him is to let things go to the devil. Coleridge certainly believes this in 1818; he protests rather too much that he already believed it in 1797. For it is to the same John Thelwall, here mocked as "Citizen John," that a very young and very unironic Coleridge then addressed his comparison between Christ, Shaftesbury, and Rousseau.

25. *The Poetical Works of Robert Southey* (Paris, 1829), p. 587.
26. Geoffrey Carnall, *Robert Southey* (London, 1964), p. 25.
27. *The Life and Correspondence of the late Robert Southey*, ed. C. C. Southey (London, 1850), 4: 186.
28. *New Letters of Robert Southey*, ed. Kenneth Curry (New York, 1965), 1: 33. The passage is from Book 12 of the *Confessions: Oeuvres complètes*, ed. Gagnebin-Raymond (Paris, 1959), 1:642.
29. Voisine, *Rousseau en Angleterre*, p. 191.
30. *Life and Correspondence*, 1: 167.
31. *Poetical Works*, p. 704.
32. Ibid., p. 632. I quote from the original and slightly different version of 1797, given in Voisine, p. 195.
33. *Life and Correspondence*, 4: 186.
34. *Quarterly Review* 16 (October 1816): 198.
35. *Edinburgh Review* 27 (December 1816): 301.
36. *The Poetical Works of Byron* (Oxford, 1960), p. 886.
37. [Eyre Evans Crowe], *Blackwood's Magazine* 11 (February 1822): 152.
38. *London Magazine* 3 (January 1821): 51.
39. *Edinburgh Review* 30 (June 1818): 87–93.
40. *London Magazine* 1 (February 1820): 124.
41. Hazlitt, *Complete Works*, 7: 304.
42. Ibid., 1: 88.
43. Ibid., p. 430n.
44. Ibid., 6: 424–425.
45. Ibid., 1: 90.
46. Ibid., 7: 52–53.
47. Ibid., 1: 89.
48. Ibid., p. 92.
49. Mme de Staël, *Oeuvres complètes*, 1: 81.
50. Hazlitt, *Complete Works*, 1: 88.
51. Coleridge, *Biographia Literaria*, chap. 4.
52. *Blackwood's Magazine* 11 (February 1822): 137.
53. Hazlitt, *Complete Works*, 1: 89.
54. Crowe, *Blackwood's Magazine* 11 (February 1822): 138.
55. Ibid., p. 145.

56. Hazlitt, *Complete Works*, 1: 90.

57. Ibid., 7: 372.

58. Ibid., pp. 365–372.

59. Thomas Moore, *Poetical Works*, ed. Thomas Moore (London, 1854), 7: 198–199.

60. Thomas Moore, *Fables for the Holy Alliance, Rhymes on the Road*, etc. (London, 1823), p. 126.

61. Thomas Moore, *Poetical Works*, 7: 345.

62. Mme d'Épinay, *Les Pseudo-Mémoires de Madame d'Épinay: Histoire de Madame de Montbrillant*, ed. Georges Roth (Paris, 1951), 1: vii–xlii.

63. *Edinburgh Review* 31 (December 1818): 48–49.

64. *Edinburgh Review* 36 (October 1821): 58.

65. *New Monthly Review*, n.s. 2 (1821): 619.

66. Ibid., p. 620.

67. Alan Lang Strout, *A Bibliography of Articles in Blackwood's Magazine, Volumes I through XVIII, 1817–1825* (Lubbock, Tex., 1959).

68. [P. G. Patmore], *Blackwood's Magazine* 4 (February 1819): 583.

69. Ibid., 5 (April 1819): 13.

70. Ibid., p. 9

71. Shelley, *Poetical Works*, p. 206.

4: SHELLEY AND ROUSSEAU

1. *Mary Shelley's Journal*, ed. Frederick L. Jones (Norman, Okla., 1947), p. 48.

2. Shelley, *Letters*, ed. Jones 1: 84.

3. *Shelley's Prose; or The Trumpet of a Prophecy*, ed. David Lee Clark (Albuquerque, N.M., 1954), p. 295.

4. Shelley, *Letters*, 1: 480.

5. Mary Shelley, "Notes on Poems of 1816," in Shelley, *Poetical Works*, p. 536.

6. Shelley, *Letters*, 1: 184.

7. Ibid., p. 51.

8. Ibid.

9. Shelley, *Prose*, p. 67.

10. Shelley, *Poetical Works*, p. 805.

11. Ibid., p. 834.

12. Shelley, *Prose*, p. 90.

13. Shelley, *Poetical Works*, p. 805.

14. *Oeuvres complètes* (1964), 3: 206.

15. David Lee Clark, "The Date and Sources of Shelley's *A Vindication of Natural Diet*," *Studies in Philology* 36 (January 1939): 70–76.

16. Shelley, *Poetical Works*, pp. 804–805.

17. Shelley, *Prose*, p. 210.

18. Ibid., p. 209. For the probable date of this essay see David Lee Clark, "Shelley's Biblical Extracts," *Modern Language Notes* 66 (November 1951): 435–441.

19. Kenneth Neill Cameron, ed., *Shelley and his Circle* (Cambridge, 1970), 3: 350.

20. Henri Peyre, *Shelley et la France* (Paris, 1935), p. 60 ff.; Voisine, *Rousseau en Angleterre*, p. 282 ff.; Donald L. Maddox, "Shelley's *Alastor* and the Legacy of Rousseau," *Studies in Romanticism* 9 (Spring 1970): 82-89.

21. Shelley, *Letters*, 1: 485.

22. Ibid., p. 486.

23. Ibid.

24. Ibid., pp. 487-488.

25. Ibid., p. 488.

26. Shelley, *Prose*, p. 292n.

27. Ibid., p. 236.

28. Shelley, *Letters*, 2: 278.

29. Ibid., p. 494.

30. Late in 1817, Shelley ordered a copy of the first discourse, insisting on an edition that contained all the responses it had provoked (*Letters*, 1: 585). And in 1818, he was carrying works of Voltaire and Rousseau across the border between France and Savoy when, because of their political significance, they were temporarily confiscated by the customs inspectors of the Kingdom of Sardinia (Newman Ivey White, *Shelley* [New York, 1947], 2:5).

31. Shelley, *Prose*, p. 164.

32. Shelley, *Letters*, 1: 482-483.

33. Shelley, *Prose*, p. 289.

34. Shelley, *Letters*, 1: 483.

35. Ibid., pp. 480-481.

36. Ibid., p. 480.

37. Ibid., p. 485.

38. Shelley, *Poetical Works*, p. 532.

39. Byron, *Works: Poetry*, ed. E. H. Coleridge (London, 1899), 2: 304-305.

40. Shelley, *Letters*, 1: 485; Byron, *Poetry*, 2: 303.

41. Rousseau, *Oeuvres complètes* (1964), 2: 519.

42. Shelley, *Poetical Works*, p. 189.

43. Shelley, *Prose*, p. 292.

44. Ibid., p. 289.

5: THE BREATH OF DARKNESS

1. G. M. Matthews, "'The Triumph of Life': a New Text," *Studia Neophilologica* 32 (1960): 271-309; Donald H. Reiman, *Shelley's "The Triumph of Life": A Critical Study* (Urbana, Ill., 1965). All quotations from the poem are taken from Reiman's edition.

2. T. S. Eliot, "What Dante Means to Me," in *To Criticize the Critic* (London, 1965), pp. 130-132.

3. Byron is the most likely source for Shelley's "the spoilers spoiled." In a letter to Murray, dated 20 May 1820, Byron alludes to an epitaph on Voltaire —*Ci-gît l'enfant gâté du monde qu'il gâta*—referring to the original as "in Grimm and Diderot." The epitaph is mentioned in Grimm's *Correspondance littéraire*, part 2, 4: 355.

4. Shelley, *Prose*, p. 293.

5. Ibid., p. 233.

6. Rousseau, *Oeuvres*, 1: 1047, 1065–1066.

7. Shelley, *Prose*, p. 174.

8. Rousseau, *Oeuvres*, 1: 1046–1047.

9. Shelley, *Letters*, 1: 482–483.

10. From Rogers, *Shelley at Work*, p. 197. In an 1819 notebook and opposite the manuscript of the "Ode to the West Wind," Shelley scribbled down the following remark of Napoleon and then characterized it as something worthy of "a rascally *cameriere di piazza*": "Rousseau: c'est pourtant lui qui a été la cause de la révolution. Au reste je ne dois pas m'en plaindre, car j'y ai attrapé le trône."

11. Shelley, *Prose*, pp. 282–283. Reverie is the perfected form of that sympathy Rousseau himself mordantly describes as stifled by intellect: "C'est la raison qui engendre l'amour propre, et c'est la réflexion qui le fortifie; C'est elle qui replie l'homme sur lui-même; c'est elle qui le sépare de tout ce qui le gêne et l'afflige: C'est la Philosophie qui l'isole; c'est par elle qu'il dit en secret, à l'aspect d'un homme souffrant, peris si tu veux, je suis en sureté. . . . On peut impunément égorger son semblable sous sa fenestre; il n'a qu'à mettre ses mains sur ses oreilles et s'argumenter un peu, pour empêcher la Nature qui se revolte en lui, de l'identifier avec celui qu'on assassine. L'homme Sauvage n'a point cet admirable talent; et faute de sagesse et de raison, on le voit toujours se livrer étourdiment au premier sentiment de l'Humanité." (*Oeuvres*, 3: 156.)

12. Cf. *Blackwood's Magazine* 5 (April 1819): 9 (See above, pp. 82–83.)

13. Rousseau, *Oeuvres*, 2: 245.

14. Ibid., 1: 1012. On page 1014 he writes, "ma destinée me rejetta dans le torrent du monde."

15. Ibid., 1: 368.

16. Edward Dowden, *Life of Shelley* (London, 1926), p. 554; A. C. Bradley, "Notes on Shelley's *Triumph of Life*," *Modern Language Review* 9 (October 1914): 450–452; Bloom, *Shelley's Mythmaking*, pp. 259–260.

17. Bradley cogently objects to Dowden's reading by making reference to a proximate and very similar passage in the "Triumph" (258–259) where "the possible success of the agents is imagined as bad." (Bradley, p. 451.)

18. Reiman, p. 169. Shelley first hit upon this word as perhaps an echo of the celebrated image with which, in the preface to the *Confessions*, Rousseau had boasted of his uniqueness: "la nature [a brisé] le moule dans lequel elle m'a jetté" (*Oeuvres*, 1: 5.)

19. Bloom, *Mythmaking*, p. 227.

20. James Rieger, *The Mutiny Within: The Heresies of Percy Bysshe Shelley* (New York, 1967), p. 207.

21. This is a peculiarity of which Shelley was proudly aware. In the preface to *Prometheus Unbound*, he writes, "The imagery which I have employed will be found, in many instances, to have been drawn from the operations of the human mind, or from those external actions by which they are expressed. This is unusual in modern poetry, although Dante and Shakespeare [and the "Greek poets"] are full of instances of the same kind."

22. From *Maria Gisborne and Edward E. Williams, Shelley's Friends: Their Journals and Letters*, ed. Frederick L. Jones (Norman, 1951) we know that Shelley was reading Chaucer very closely toward the end of his life: entry of

18 November 1821: "read some of Chaucer with S."; entry of 20 December 1821: "Passed the evening at S's. He read aloud Chaucer's dream—a poem of the finest feeling." A reference to "Chaucer's dream" in the early nineteenth century is undoubtedly a reference to "The Book of the Duchess." I am indebted to Professor Howard Schless of Columbia University for pointing out to me that the 1721 Urry edition of Chaucer did, in fact, present the title of this work as "The Dream of Chaucer."

23. Earl Wasserman has brilliantly elucidated how the mimesis of developing consciousness is a recurring strategy in Shelley's poetry. Cf. his article on "Adonais," "Progressive Revelation as a Poetic Mode," *ELH* 21 (1954): 274–326, and in his *The Subtler Language* (Baltimore, 1959); and the following about *Epipsychidion*: "in [its] first movement, nearly all the essential images and themes of the poem have been deposited in disarray, and the succeeding stages will be successive efforts to draw upon that pool of elements and organize them into a stable, meaningful, and satisfying pattern of relationships" (*Shelley, A Critical Reading* [Baltimore, 1971], p. 430).

24. Goethe, *Werke*, ed. Erich Trunz (Hamburg, 1949), 3: 40, ll. 1084–1091.

25. G. M. Matthews, "On Shelley's 'The Triumph of Life,'" p. 115n. Since writing this, I have discovered that Robinson, *Shelley and Byron* has already pointed out how Shelley transformed the lines from *Faust*. The significance that Professor Robinson attributes to this change (pp. 222 ff.) is different from my own.

26. *The Letters of John Keats*, ed. Hyder Rollins (Cambridge, 1958), 1: 193–194.

27. W. B. Yeats, *Essays and Introductions* (New York, 1961), pp. 88 ff., 94.

28. Shelley, *Prose*, p. 67.

29. Ibid., p. 293.

30. Rousseau, *Oeuvres*, 2: 1228–1229.

31. On 26 May 1820, Mary Shelley requested of Hunt that he "select one of the later Indicators and send it by the Post." (Shelley, *Letters*, 2: 201) On 12 July of the same year, Shelley himself asked Peacock to send "Indicators and whatever else you may think interesting." (*Letters*, 2: 214) Shelley must have enjoyed the Hunt weekly because in October of 1821 (only months away from the writing of "The Triumph of Life") he asked the editor to bring him "a perfect copy of the Indicator." (*Letters*, 2: 356).

32. Leigh Hunt, "Rousseau's Pygmalion," *The Indicator* 1 (London, 1812 reprint): p. 241.

33. Ibid., p. 241.

34. Ibid., pp. 241–242.

35. Moritz Retzsch, *Extracts from Goethe's tragedy of Faustus, explanatory of the plates by Retsch [sic], intended to illustrate that work* (London, 1820).

36. Shelley, *Letters*, 2: 407.

37. Ibid.

38. Rousseau, *Oeuvres*, 2: 146–147.

39. Thomas Mann, "Goethe's Faust" (1938), *Essays of Three Decades*, trans. H. T. Lowe-Porter (New York, 1947), p. 36.

40. Rousseau, *Oeuvres*, 1: 320–322.

41. Ibid., 320.

42. Ibid.

43. Shelley, *Prose*, p. 233.

44. Shelley, is here indebted to the lines from "The Ballad of Patrick Spence" which Coleridge used as an epigraph to "Dejection":

> Late, late yestreen I saw the new Moon,
> With the old Moon in her arms;
> And I fear, my Mother dear!
> We shall have a deadly storm.

See S. T. Coleridge, *Complete Poetical Works*, ed. Ernest Hartley Coleridge (Oxford, 1912), 1: 362.

45. Shelley, *Prose*, p. 67. Shelley was not yet twenty when he wrote this.

46. Shelley, *Poetical Works*, pp. 417 ff.

47. Bloom, *Mythmaking*, p. 238.

48. "The Triumph of Life" is thus an anticipation of Marshall McLuhan's thesis that Western typographic man has overdefined himself according to the visual sense. Cf. *The Gutenberg Galaxy* (Toronto, 1962).

49. How an imagination repressed by intellect will take its revenge as terror is a theme James Rieger (*The Mutiny Within*, p. 127 and *passim*) demonstrates as informing not only Mary's *Frankenstein* but likewise the novels of her father and the poems of her husband.

50. One of the best and most succinct descriptions of the constants in Shelley's symbolic universe is to be found in Donald Reiman's introduction to his edition of the "Triumph," pp. 8–18.

51. *Shelley and Synesthesia* (Evanston, Ill., 1964).

52. For an awareness of the kinaesthetic in Shelley, I am indebted to R. H. Fogle, *The Imagery of Keats and Shelley* (Hamden, 1949).

53. *Theogony* ll. 160 ff. Cf. Hjalmar Frisk, *Griechisches Etymologishes Wörterbuch* (Heidelberg, 1973), vol. 1.

54. Shelley, *Prose*, pp. 291–293.

55. Reiman, *Triumph*, p. 83.

56. Shelley, Prose, p. 295.

57. Matthews construes this first part of the line as "Dances i' the wind." This reading, while it replaces the suggestive "east" with a redundant and nonfunctional "wind," does bring into the lines the poem's very important motif of song and dance. Merely on general grounds, "dances" seems a better word than the more generic "moves." Moreover, as Reiman admits (p. 189), "moves" is canceled in manuscript and "dances" is not. The phrase "i' the wind" that Matthews attaches to "dance" is, however, canceled. As poetry, both Shelley cancellations seem eminently dispensable. But apparently Matthews agrees with Reiman that "one must use some canceled word (either 'Moves' or 'wind')" (p. 189). Although I have absolutely no competence in editorial matters, I would suggest that an eclectic but totally uncanceled reading—"Dances i' the east" or "Dances up the east"— works perhaps better as poetry. The passage is attempting to bring into concentrated focus all the imagery of the poem as a whole; and the inclusion of both the dance and the dawn motifs would seem to be desirable.

58. Shelley, *Letters*, 2: 339.

POSTSCRIPT

1. Ernst Cassirer, *The Philosophy of the Enlightenment* (Boston, 1955).
2. Ibid., p. 104. The French text is from Condillac, *Oeuvres philosophiques*, ed. Georges LeRoy (Paris, 1947), 1: 357-358. It occurs in part 2, chapter 2 of the *Traité des animaux.*
3. Cassirer, *Philosophy of Enlightenment*, p. 103.
4. Eliot, *To Criticize the Critic*, pp. 130-132.
5. I think especially of the idea of Shelley given in Harold Bloom's *Yeats* (New York, 1970).
6. Ivor Winters, *In Defense of Reason* (Denver, 1937), p. 459. Oddly enough, the same kind of criticism is applicable to Shelley appreciators of the "ineffectual angel" persuasion, that unfortunate characterization of the poet whom Matthew Arnold considered "incoherent Shelley."
7. Cf. the Shelley chapter in F. R. Leavis, *Revaluation: Tradition and Development in English Poetry* (New York, 1963).

Index

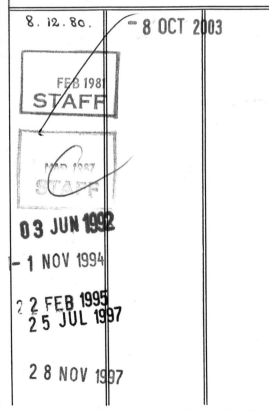